When You Travel

by

Ezell Pittman, PhD

When You Travel
All rights reserved
ISBN-13:
978-1537774350
ISBN-10:
1537774352

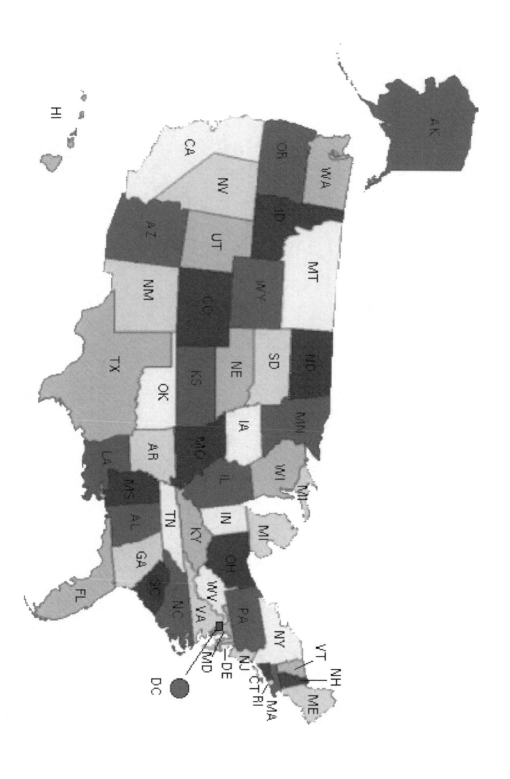

The World

Table of Contents

Acknowledgments					
Introduction					
Introductory Essay					
State	Pg	State	Pg	State	Pg
AL 1		AK...............8		AZ 14	
AR 20		CA 26		CO 35	
CT..............41		DE 47		FL 51	
GA..............61		HI 70		ID...............74	
IL 77		IN 84		IA...............90	
KS..............94		KY 99		LA 104	
ME...........110		MD 115		MA 121	
MI...........129		MN 135		MS...........140	
MO 146		MT............153		NE 158	
NV 163		NH............168		NJ 172	
NM 179		NY 184		NC 193	
ND............200		OH............205		OK............214	
OR 220		PA..............224		RI...............233	
SC.............237		SD..............248		TN 252	
TX 261		UT 271		VT 275	
VA...........279		WA...........288		WV 293	
WI.............299		WY 304		*DC 308	

Contents (Continued)

Canada	338
Mexico	345
Central America	352
Caribbean	357
Continents	368
Africa	370
Antarctica	377
Asia	382
Australia	392
Europe	397
North America	405
South America	410
World Heritage Sites	414
Oceans	416
Seven Wonders of the World	419
Geographic Superlatives	422
Epilogue	428

ACKNOWLEDGMENTS

I thank my creator who directed and guided my path as I wrote this guide because I did not have a plan to write it. To my granddaughter Courtney B. Pittman, I really appreciate your help with the manuscript because as you know, I did not have a clue as to where to begin. Because of the way this project began, I am reminded of this saying about planning for the future: "Whatever you can do, or dream you can, begin it because boldness has genius, power and magic in it." Remember, too, when it comes to realizing your dream, the forces for you are greater than the forces against you.

To Dr. Bobby Donald, who read *From This Road* and this manuscript and connected the dots in my life in his introductory essay as no one could, thank you.

To Lorenza Breedlove, who was president of the Ridgewood Foundation when I was selected to serve as the travel coordinator; to the late Mamie G. Floyd, educator and community activist; and to Deborah Breedlove, all of whom served as the first travel guides prior to my tenure as coordinator, thank you for the opportunity to learn more about travel than I ever knew.

To Jerlean Noble, author and president of the Columbia Writers Alliance, thank you for guiding me through the tunnel and helping me make this book a reality.

To Alenda Jones, who edited my book, I thank you for being tireless in your efforts to get it right.

To all who have traveled the world with me during the past twenty years, thank you for making it possible for me to write this guide. I hope you will find it useful during your future travels.

To all of my middle school geography teachers, high school history and social studies teachers, and especially to the late Lloyd T. Blatch, who taught me history in undergraduate school, you were my inspiration to write this guide.

"The way to get the most out of life is to look at it as an adventure." --Author Unknown

INTRODUCTION

Often I am asked about places to go and sites to see in the United States, so I decided to write this step-by-step travel guide. It will, I hope, suggest attractions to visit, no matter where you plan to travel in the world. When I was travel coordinator for the Ridgewood Foundation, a non-profit organization, in Columbia, South Carolina, I planned trips that included visits to African American sites. I had to research them because they were not listed in the mainstream travel magazines. I have noted in this guide sites to visit for those interested in African American history.

According to the National Register of Historic Places of the National Park Service, there are over 800 places in 42 states and two U. S. territories that have played a role in African American history; only a few are listed here. I was amazed to learn in my research about banks, cemeteries, clubs, colleges, forts, homes, hospitals, schools and other places that played a role in the African American experience. **Note:** An asterisk herein indicates the site is **African American.**

Furthermore, I included the names of well-known natives or residents of each state, some of whom lived in the 18th century or earlier, and areas where they performed, served or contributed. One of the most revealing facts was the number of people who were civil rights activists or were activists in some capacity. Also, I included facts of interest, notable attractions, and summary comments on my personal travel experiences or note of historical information.

This is a travel guide that lists many places to consider when you travel, but it will serve as a lesson in history and geography as well. There are a number of things that we do that would be considered geographic, such as choosing a place to visit on holidays and vacation and planning how to get there. Geography helps us find our way in a strange city or find our car in a parking lot.

Geographic knowledge enables us to understand things we do on a daily or other episodic basis.

The word *geography* was invented by the Greek scholar Eratosphenes and literally means "writing about the earth." The word can be divided into two parts: ge- and -graphy. *Ge-* means "the earth," and *-graphy* refers to writing. Of course, *geography* today means much more than writing about the earth. A typical definition today reads, "The science of earth's physical features, resources, climates, populations, etc."

Eratosthenes, "the Father of Geography," was born around 276 B.C.E. (Before Common Era) in Cyrene, Libya. Without Eratosthenes, Ptolemy, Alexander von Humboldt, and many other important geographers, important and essential discoveries, world exploration and expansion, and advancing technologies would not have taken place.

Information in my book *From This Road* reveals my interest in geography and exploration. My first trip outside of the Florida area was to New York after my freshman year in college. I was mesmerized by the vibrant metropolis. I visited museums, art galleries, and parks where there were concerts. On one weekend I boarded a bus and went to New Haven, CT, and walked around the beautiful campus of Yale University. On another weekend I went to Boston and Cambridge, Massachusetts, and explored the campus of Harvard and MIT because I realized my lack of exposure both culturally and educationally.

Another trip chronicled in the book was my second trip to California after my military tour and later a trip to Europe with educators from New York. When I was asked in 1993 to coordinate the Ridgewood Foundation's travel program, it was the beginning of my domestic traveling experience. While we did not plan to visit the lower 48 states, Mexico and Eastern Canada, we traveled to places mentioned in Dr. Martin Luther King, Jr.'s, "I Have A Dream" speech.

We went to the prodigious hilltops of New Hampshire.

We saw the mighty mountains of New York.

We went to the Alleghenies of Pennsylvania.

We saw the snow-capped Rockies of Colorado.

We saw the curvaceous slopes of California.

We were near Stone Mountain in Georgia.

We saw the Smoky Mountains of Tennessee.

We saw Pike's Peak in Colorado that inspired Katherine Lee Bates to write "America the Beautiful."

We saw amber waves of grain.

We traveled from coast-to-coast and from "sea to shining sea."

My international travel began with a trip to West Africa in 1994, the first of my five visits to the continent. In Accra and Cape Coast, we saw a moving ceremony called "The Door of No Return." Slaves were taken from there to North America. The stench of the holding cells still lingers after hundreds of years.

To cruise on the Nile, the longest river in the world (4,000 miles), for three days from Luxor to Aswan was the ultimate cruise experience. From this trip was travel around the world to six continents and fifty countries. It all started *From This Road*, where I grew up in Jacob, FL. "You Can Get Anywhere From Here" is the motto of Midlands Technical College in Columbia, SC. This is right because you can travel anywhere from where you are. This volume delves further into my interest in geography and travel around the world and reveals the knowledge I have gained through these experiences.

Along with the historical part of the guide, I hope this volume will give you a different perspective on places when you travel. I especially hope it will help you travel with a purpose and serve as a guide to monuments, museums, birthplaces, and sites important to African-American history.

Lastly, before you join me on my journey, I want to make this note: This volume contains a lot of data from various sources. What I have reported is the most reliable information obtainable as I was doing my research. Having said that, safe travels and enjoy the journey.

Introductory Essay

Bobby J. Donaldson, PhD

Columbia, South Carolina

"You will never know where the road will lead."

As a professor of history, I am very pleased to write an introductory essay for Dr. Ezell Pittman's latest travel volume. My path crossed Dr. Pittman's a few years ago in Columbia, South Carolina, and I was immediately taken by his indefatigable energy, his immense knowledge of history, and his exuberant (indeed contagious) passion for travel.

In Dr. Pittman's memoir entitled *From This Road*, he notes that his goal when escorting "a travel group is to educate and broaden their horizons." The pages before us continue this invaluable mission - one of teaching and expanding the worldview of readers. With meticulous and insightful detail, Dr. Pittman's latest book highlights his encyclopedic knowledge of travel destinations across the United States and around the world.

Culling from an extensive travelogue and research, Pittman has compiled a readable and intriguing catalogue of important facts, notable landmarks, and influential personalities.

What an audacious undertaking this is! After years of leading groups to travel destinations around the world, Dr. Pittman now shares his insightful advice with a wider reading public.

From the small confines of a sharecropping family living near a sawmill town in Florida's panhandle, Ezell Pittman has explored nearly every corner of the world. In a community, framed by struggle and determination, Pittman looked beyond the small spaces of Jacob City and Port St. Joe, Florida. In previous writings, Pittman remarked: "The dirt road I first traveled in Jacob was the first step to my traveling many roads around the world."

A child of the Great Depression, Ezell Pittman was born in Jacob City, Florida, a three square mile African American enclave of a few hundred residents. In looking at the bold and resolute steps Dr. Pittman took to expand his education, to advance his career, and to deepen his travel experience, it seems as though he took seriously the biblical instruction that he learned from Saint Mary Missionary Baptist Church in Jacob City, Zion Fair Baptist Church in Port St. Joe, and Second Baptist Church in Jacksonville: "And do not be conformed to this world, but be transformed by the renewing of your mind" (Romans 12:2).

As I read about Dr. Pittman's transformation and his fascination with travel and exploration, nearly every page of this book compelled me to pause and think of other historical references, publications, and individuals who championed travel and tourism.

One of the earliest American travelogues came at the hands of French traveler and author Alexis De Tocqueville. De Tocqueville and a colleague arrived in New York City in May 1831. Eager to learn more about the customs and geography of the emerging democratic nation, the two men traveled vast stretches of the United States by steamboat, stagecoach, horseback, and canoes for nearly nine months through seventeen states. After returning to France in February 1832, De Tocqueville published *Democracy in America*. The volume, steeped in local lore and reflections on history, culture, and values, immediately became a bestseller and remains a widely read text today. Since the publication of *Democracy in America*, the nation's fascination with expansion, travel, and adventure has spawned scores of publications. Fortuitously, Dr. Pittman's volume adds substantive new angles, context, and background that complement existing literature. Readers will see that Dr. Pittman's extensive knowledge of African American history makes this book a much more inclusive and diverse publication than many of its peers.

When Pittman was born in the Florida panhandle, in the *New York Times* there was a curious and rather prophetic column entitled "Negro Travel Tide is Rising." The reporter wrote: "Negro Americans in increasing numbers are taking to the crowded travel lanes leading to Europe, prompted by the desire to observe and study cultural and social development in the Old World and by the prospect of enjoying a variety of recreational opportunities" (*New York Times*, July 19, 1936).

Curiously, months after the *New York Times* extolled the virtues of international travel in the midst of the Great Depression, Rachel A. Austin, a field worker for the Federal Writers Project Negro Unit, traveled to the campus of Edward Waters College, an institution in Jacksonville where Ezell Pittman would later attend for a short time. Austin visited the school to speak to the college's elderly watchman, Samuel Simeon Andrews, affectionately known by students and faculty as Parson.

Parson Andrews was born into slavery in Macon, Georgia, on November 18, 1850. Raised in Sparta, Andrews was then purchased by Lewis Ripley of Beaufort, South Carolina, and later sold to other slave-owners. When Austin asked Andrews to reflect on his memories growing up, he remembered the troubles and horrors experienced in slavery, the "great rejoicing" of Emancipation, his career as a preacher, and his labors on the Florida Railroad when he traveled up and down the Atlantic Coast. As Andrews looked back over his long life, he recalled his heroic efforts to save a passenger involved in a deadly train crash in the late 1880s. He noted that the train company "gave me a free pass for life with which I rode all over the United States and once into Canada." He proudly showed Austin the worn pass that he received for his valiant assistance. Eager to "travel over the United States again," Parson Andrews, a spry eighty-five year old, lamented that his active schedule at the school and in church compelled him to stay close to home.

Following in the tradition of Parson Andrews, this book, written by a former Edwards College student, provided readers a travel pass - one adeptly written by an expert with years of training and reflection. When Pittman was fourteen years old, the *New York Amsterdam News* carried an intriguing column that read: "Travel agent is an expert in his field, just as the lawyer or the doctor. He trained to solve the problems that arise when people leave home and start crossing borders. Geographer, traffic expert, economist, linguist, he is all of these in addition to having an expert knowledge of international immigration law and custom requirements."

In so many respects, Dr. Pittman's prodigious research and his lengthy record as a travel consultant and tour coordinator demonstrate how he continues to fit a job description crafted over sixty-five years ago!

Indeed, the work at hand continues a long legacy. As I reviewed Dr. Pittman's valuable volume, I reflected upon the pioneering work of other inveterate champions of travel. As Ezell Pittman prepared to graduate from New Stanton High School in Jacksonville, he learned the regrettable news that the school's scheduled commencement speaker, Dr. Mary McLeod Bethune, passed away one week before graduation.

Born in rural Sumter County, South Carolina, Bethune founded a school for girls in 1904 in Daytona Beach. As an educator, civil leader, and fundraiser, Bethune kept a busy itinerary. In the 1930s, Bethune published a column in the *Pittsburg Courier* entitled "From Day to Day." Frequently, she offered readers detailed accounts of her travels and observations. In April 1951, as Bethune traveled across the country by train and airplane raising money for the United Negro College Fund, she reminded her readers: "Often as I looked down upon my country from its spacious skies as the great planes fly over its air lanes, I never go aloft that I do not feel anew the bigness and the richness of America and its cultures (*Chicago Defender*, May 12, 1951).

Others steadfastly agreed with Bethune. After a stint in World War I and service as a postal employee, Victor Hugo Green embarked on a highly successful travel-publishing career based in Harlem, New York - only a short distance from where Pittman would stay when he studied at Columbia University. Green wanted to provide African American travelers a "vacation without aggregation." In the face of humiliation and personal indignities in segregated facilities, Green published *The Negro Motorist Green Book: A Travel Guide*. Later editions included "Landmarks of Negro History." The famous *Green Book* sought "to give the Negro traveler information that will keep him from running into difficulties, embarrassments and to make his trip more enjoyable." The *New York Amsterdam News* applauded the publication as "the beacon light for the traveler and vacationists in the United States - the main instrument in making the Negro's travel more pleasant" (*Amsterdam News*, June 19, 1954).

The acclaimed Langston Hughes was an astute "traveler and vacationist." In Hughes' autobiography, *I Wander as I Wander*, he writes of his life's journey from 1930 to 1937. Each of his destinations was a place of discovery and personal inquiry. And each trip compelled the famous poet to look inward to assess his own values, ambitions and limitations. Hughes notes: "Most of my life from childhood on has been spent moving, traveling, changing places, knowing people in one school, in one town or in one group, or on one ship a little while, but soon never seeing most of them again." In other publications, Hughes regularly reflected on how travel shaped his writings and cultural worldview.

On January 28, 1965, Langston Hughes penned an essay in the *Chicago Defender* entitled

"Memories of Travels Abroad." Reflecting upon his excursions and visits across the world, Hughes recalled: "Sometimes I think I have a postcard mind - remembering visually years later the colors of seas and mountains and skies I never thought I would know before St. Christopher, the patron saint of travel, safely took me to them.

Like Dr. Bethune, Victor Green, and Langston Hughes, Ezell Pittman's life has been shaped by the "bigness and the richness of America." The author of this work has a "post card mind," and he provides readers a detailed and captivating account of landmarks, stories, historical vignettes, and useful lessons.

Although Dr. Pittman's travels include many destinations across the wide expanses of our nation, he saw first-hand the inherent barriers and hurdles. When Pittman traveled from Oakland, California, to Columbia, South Carolina, on a Greyhound bus in 1961, he came face-to-face with the biting realities of racial segregation. When denied services at a restaurant and told to go to a take-out window, Pittman and a companion refused to abide by the dictates of the time and went to a nearby grocery store to purchase provisions. Indeed, despite pronounced barriers and challenges over a lifetime, Pittman worked hard to transcend many personal and professional boundaries. And this drive, determination, and thirst for new adventures and opportunities are readily evident in this volume.

Pittman's book highlights an inquisitive mind eager to know more about the mysteries and wonders of the broad world around him. Following the example of noted author Maya Angelou, Pittman regards travel as a "passport to understanding," an exercise by which individuals widen their perspective about the world as they develop deeper self-awareness and introspection.

When You Travel is an accessible, readable reference source. It is both inspirational and informative, a volume designed for those who seek to discover, grow, and explore. Trained as a psychological counselor, career consultant, and educator, Pittman piques interest and curiosity. He seeks to inspire others to move beyond the safe and predictable confines of their local environment and to explore culture and history in new destinations.

From a dirt road in rural Florida, the feet of this daring dreamer have touched the soil of nearly every corner of the world. Drawing upon years of experience with the Ridgewood Foundation in Columbia, South Carolina, and other organizations, Pittman channels his travels towards these pages as he guides readers from place to place. Under Dr. Pittman's leadership, the Foundation explored 48 continental states, Eastern Canada and Mexico. Travelers came from Delaware, Georgia, Florida, Maryland, New York, South Carolina and Virginia.

Admirably, this work illuminates little known or explored locations and sites. It is at once an encyclopedia and a travelogue. Replete with personal reflections and memories, this remarkable book offers a traveler useful tourist tips and insightful historical information. As detailed as it is, readers should be reminded that this work is a subjective exercise, the results of careful research and fact finding, and yet it is the perspective on the nation and the world through the lens of one individual. Like Jack Kerouac, Mark Twain, Langston Hughes, and Mary McLeod Bethune, Pittman's prose paints a vivid and arresting picture of the world, one that beckons readers to step onto the pages. As you will read, Pittman's world is shaped by common threads, intriguing vistas, rich tapestries, and divergent paths. Pittman's world is one of bustling cities, small towns, undiscovered spots of the beaten path, popular attractions, historical destinations, diverse personalities, and curious local landmarks. The world that Pittman chronicles here in meticulous detail awaits all who seek to "broaden their horizons."

ALABAMA

22nd State / December 14, 1819 /
Rank in area sq. miles: 30

Nickname: Heart of Dixie, Camellia State

Capital: Montgomery

Most populous cities: Birmingham, Montgomery, Mobile

Attractions: First White House of the Confederacy, Civil Rights Memorial*, Alabama Shakespeare Festival, in Montgomery; Ivy Green (Helen Keller's birthplace in Tuscumbia), Barber

1

Vintage Motor Sports Museum, Civil Rights Institute*, Vulcan Park and Museum (world's largest cast iron statue), in Birmingham; G.W. Carver Interpretive Museum*, in Tuskegee; W.C. Handy Home, Museum and Library*, Frank Lloyd Wright's Rosenbaum House, in Florence; U.S. Space & Rocket Ctr., in Huntsville; U.S. Alabama Memorial Park, Army Aviation Museum at Fort Rucker; Brown Chapel AME Church*, Edmund Pettus Bridge, in Selma; Tuskegee Institute National Historic Site*, Sixteenth Street Baptist Church, Kelly Ingram Park, in Birmingham; W.C. Handy Birthplace, Museum, and Library*, in Florence

Places to visit and things to see in the most populous cities:

Birmingham - Birmingham Civil Rights Institute*, Sixteenth Street Baptist Church, Kelly Ingram Park*, Alabama Sports Hall of Fame,

Alabama Jazz Hall of Fame, Eddie Kendrick Memorial Park*

Montgomery - Dexter Avenue King Memorial Baptist Church*, Montgomery Museum of Fine Arts, Rosa Parks Library and Museum*, National Center for the Study of Civil Rights and African American Culture at Alabama State University*, State Capitol

Mobile - USS Alabama Memorial Park, Mobile Bay, Hank Aaron Stadium, Gulf Coast Exploreum

Well-known Alabamians and residents:

Percy Julian - Medical Professional, Chemist, Scientist (1899-1975)

Jesse Owens - Track and Field Athlete (1913-1980)

Mae C. Jemison - Doctor, Astronaut (1956-)

W. C. Handy - Songwriter (1873-1958)

Rosa Parks - Civil Rights Activist (1913-2005)

Zora Neal Hurston - Author, Civil Rights Activist (1891-1960)

Fred Shuttlesworth - Civil Rights Activist, Minister (1922-2011)

John Lewis - Civil Rights Activist - U. S. Representative (1940-)

Coretta Scott King - Writer, Women's Rights Activist, Anti-War Activist, Civil Rights Activist (1927-2006)

Ralph D. Abernathy - Civil Rights Activist, Minister (1926-1990)

Nate King Cole - Film Actor, Singer, Pianist, Television Actor, Television Personality (1919-1965)

Hank Aaron - Civil Rights Activist, Base Ball Player (1934-)

Octavia Spencer - Film Actress, Television Actress (1972-)

Joe Lewis - Boxer (1914-1981)

Morris Dees - Civil Rights Activist, Lawyer (1936-)

Hellen Keller - Educator, Journalist (1880-1968)

Frank M. Johnson - Civil Rights Activist, Lawyer, Judge (1918-1999)

Harper Lee - Author (1926-2016)

Interesting Information

- The Confederate flag was first designed and flown in Alabama.

- Alabama workers built the first rocket to put humans on the moon.

- Alabama introduced Mardi Gras to the Western world.

- The Alabama Department of Archives is the oldest state-funded archival agency in the nation.

*****

Alabama is the home of the first White House of the Confederacy in Montgomery as well as the U.S. Space and Rocket Center in Huntsville. I often tell travelers to visit Montgomery because it lays claim to being the home of the Modern Civil Rights Movement. The Montgomery bus boycott of 1955, sparked by Mrs. Rosa Parks, helped launch the movement. The Dexter Avenue King Memorial Baptist Church in Montgomery, where Dr. Martin Luther King, Jr. was pastor, led the movement. Other confrontations occurred at Birmingham in 1963 and in Selma in 1965. Brown Chapel AME Church is in Selma and was associated with the 1965 voting rights campaign of the Southern Christian Leadership Conference (SCLC). Another attraction is Tuskegee University, which was founded by Booker T. Washington. Two of the campus attractions are the George Washington Carver Museum and the General Daniel "Chappie" James Aerospace Center. Booker T. Washington and Dr. George Washington Carver are buried on the campus. The Tuskegee Airmen National Site at Moton Field is in Tuskegee. Moton Field is the site of pilot training for the Tuskegee Airmen. The field is named for Robert Russa Moton, second president of Tuskegee. Because of its history, I believe places and paths of the Civil Rights Movement in Alabama should be considered as destinations for travelers.

.

ALASKA

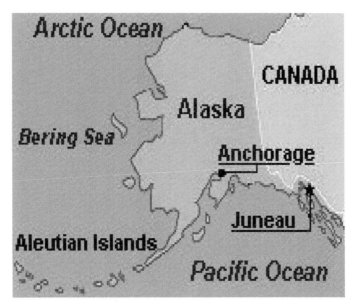

49th State / January 3, 1959 / Rank in area sq. miles: 1

Nickname: The Last Frontier, Land of the Midnight Sun

Capital: Juneau

Most populous cities: Anchorage, Fairbanks, Juneau

Attractions: Portage Glacier, in Chugach National Forest; Mendenhall Glacier, in Tongass National

Forest; Totem Heritage Center, in Ketchikan; Glacier Bay National Park and Preserve; Mt. Denali (North America's highest peak), in Denali National Park and Preserve; Mt. Roberts Tramway, in Juneau; Alaska Maritime National Wildlife Refuge; St. Michael's Cathedral, Alaska Raptor Center, in Sitka; White Pass, a Yukon Route railroad, in Skagway; Katmai National Park and Preserve; University of Alaska Museum of the North, in Fairbanks.

Things to see and places to visit in the most populous cities:

Anchorage - Iditarod Sled Dog Race (Ceremonial Start), Anchorage Museum at Rasmussen Center, Kenai Fjords National Park, Alaska Native Heritage Center

Fairbanks - Fountainhead Antique Auto Museum, Running Deer Ranch, University of Alaska Museum of the North, University of Alaska Fairbanks,

Pioneer Air Museum, Salmon Bake at Pioneer Park, 1st Alaska Outdoor School

Juneau - Mendenhall Glacier, Whale Watching, Glacier Gardens Rainforest Adventure, Salmon Hatchery, Alaska State Museum, Gold Creek Salmon Bake

Well-known Alaskans and residents:

Charles Mingus - Civil Rights Activist, Pianist, Guitarist, Songwriter (1922-1979)

Susan Butcher - Pioneer in Sled-Dog Racing (1954-2006)

Curt Schilling - Baseball Player (1966-)

Interesting Information

- Alaska is more than twice as big as Texas.
- The state of Rhode Island could fit into Alaska 425 times.
- Nearly one-third of Alaska lies within the Arctic Circle.

- Alaska is the biggest state, but it has the fewest people.

- Many people use planes to travel in Alaska.

- Mt. Denali, the highest mountain in the U.S. (20,321 ft.), is in Alaska.

- The sun stays up for 24 hours on the first day of summer in Barrow, Alaska. On the first day of winter, it does not rise at all.

- The Trans-Alaska Pipeline moves up to 88,000 barrels of oil per hour on its 800 mile journey from Prudhoe Bay to Valdez.

- The state's coastline extends over 6,000 miles.

- Seventeen of the 20 highest peaks in the United States are located in Alaska.

*****

Of the 50 states I have visited, I would say Alaska is one of the most interesting. There is nothing quite like seeing the last frontier. My first visit was on a cruise ship, and my second was a land tour. Alaska is a land with incredible scenic beauty, wide-open spaces, and abundant wildlife.

Travel in Alaska is unlike anywhere else. Flightseeing is a popular tourist activity; private air carriers provide wilderness and glacier tours. The locals' favorite form of traveling is by sea. The Alaska Marine Highway System (AMHS) is an affordable, informal option to reach 25 ports of call in the state. A majority of the cities and villages of Alaska are only accessible by air or sea.

Another Alaskan attraction is the Iditarod. It is a spectacular race and one of the greatest endurance tests in sports. Starting from Anchorage in March and ending in a week or two in Nome, competitors mush sled dogs across 1,150 miles of snow and ice. When I visited, we were given a demonstration of the sled dogs and racing in the Iditarod.

Lastly, I love panoramic views and tall mountains. The most spectacular view was Mt.

Denali, standing at 20,320 feet, as the tallest peak in North America. Mt. Denali's indigenous name is *Athabascans*, which means "the high one." Alaska is an adventure you do not want to miss!

ARIZONA

48th State / February 14, 1912 / Rank in area sq. miles: 6

Nickname: Grand Canyon State

Capital: Phoenix

Most populous cities: Phoenix, Tucson, Mesa

Attractions: Grand Canyon; Painted Desert, in Grand Canyon and Petrified Forest National Parks; Glen Canyon National Recreation Area; Canyon de Chelly National Monument; meteor Crater, near Winslow; London Bridge, Lake Havasu City; Biosphere 2, Oracle; Navajo National Monument;

Tombstone, a historic mining town; Tempe Town Lake

Things to see and places to visit in the most populous cities:

Phoenix - Arizona State University Planetarium, Heritage Square, Phoenix Art Museum, Hall of Fame Fire Museum, Arizona Science Center, Desert Botanical Garden, Arizona State Capitol Museum

Tucson - Arizona Sonora Desert Museum, El Presidio Historic District, Pima Air and Space Museum, University of Arizona in Tucson, St. Augustine Cathedral, International Wildlife Museum

Mesa - Commemorative Air Force Museum, Arizona Museum of Natural History, Arizona Museum for Youth, Buckhorn Wildlife Museum

Well-known Arizonians and residents:

Elgie Batteau - Educator (1905-1994)

Clovis Campbell, Sr. - State Legislator (1930-2004)

Fred Snowden - Basketball Coach (1936-1994)

Barry M. Goldwater - U.S. Senator, Businessman (1909-1998)

Lynda Carter - Film Actress, Songwriter (1951-)

Cesar Chavez - Activist (1927-1993)

Barbara Eden - Film Actress, Television Actress, Singer (1931-)

Linda Ronstadt - Singer (1946-)

Stewart Udall - U.S. Congressman (1920-2010)

Emma Stone - Film Actress (1988-)

Frank Lloyd Wright - Architect (1867-1959)

Interesting Information

- Arizona is one of the Four Corner States noted as the spot in the United States where a person can stand in four corners at the same time (Colorado, New Mexico and Utah are the other three).

- Oraibi is the oldest Indian settlement in the United States.

- Tombstone, Ruby, Gillette, and Gunsight are among the ghost towns scattered throughout the state.

- A fountain believed to be the tallest in the world is located in Fountain, Arizona.

- The world's largest canyon is the Grand Canyon in Arizona.

- The Grand Canyon is 227 miles long, 1 mile deep, and has an average width of 10 miles.

- Kingman, Arizona, is the home to the longest stretch (about 158 miles) of old U.S. Route 66 still in existence.

- The sun shines in southern Arizona 85% of the time, which is considerably more sunshine than Florida or Hawaii.

- Among all the states, Arizona has the largest percentage of its land designated as Indian lands.

- The world's largest telescope is at Kitt Peak National Observatory, Arizona.

- Yuma claims to be the sunniest place in the United States. The sun shines for an average of 11 hours a day.

*****

As a native of Florida, I like Arizona for its warm climate - especially in some areas during the winter. Of course, Arizona is the Grand Canyon State. For those who are adventuresome, you can now walk on an exhilarating 70 feet-long glass bottomed Grand Canyon Skywalk, which juts 4,000 feet above the canyon floor. Arizona is a great destination for resort vacations, a horseback safari, or a work-stint at a dude ranch.

When I traveled to Arizona, we visited the living-history town of Tombstone (Boot Hill). This town shed light onto Arizona's rugged characters, such as Billy Clanton, Frank McLaury, and Tom McLaury, who were killed during the famed gunfight at the O.K. Corral. Perhaps when you think of Arizona images, what comes to mind is the Old West, cowboys, Indians, deserts, cacti - things straight out of TV Westerns. When you visit the Grand Canyon, and I encourage you to see this awesome view, spectacular things await you.

ARKANSAS

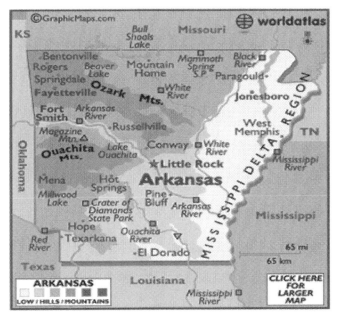

25th State / June 15, 1836 / Rank in area sq. miles: 29

Nickname: The Natural State, Razorback State

Capital: Little Rock

Most populous cities: Little Rock, Ft. Smith, Fayetteville

Attractions: Eureka Springs; Ozark Folk Center State Park, in Mountain View; Blanchard Springs Caverns, in Ozark National Forest; Crater of

Diamond State Park, in Murfreesboro; Toltec Mounds Archeological State Park, in Scott; Buffalo National River; Hot Springs National Park; Pea Ridge National Military Park; William J. Clinton Presidential Library and Museum; Little Rock Central High School National Historic Site, in Little Rock; Chrysler Bridges Museum of American Art, in Bentonville

Little Rock - Home of the "Little Rock Nine" and Central High School, The William J. Clinton Presidential Center, The Clinton Library (President Clinton was born in Hope, AR), River Market District, the Capitol Building, The Governor's Mansion, The Old Mill (North Little Rock), Riverfront Park

Ft. Smith - Ft. Smith Museum of History, Ft. Smith Air Museum

Fayetteville - Old Main or University Hall, University of Arkansas, Clinton House Museum

(First home of Bill and Hillary Clinton), Walton's Five and Dime (Sam Walton's original store is in Rogers, AR.)

Well-known Arkansans and residents:

Sister Rosetta Tharpe - Singer (1915-1973)

Louis Jordan - Singer, Saxophonist (1907-1975)

Daisy Bates - Publisher, Civil Rights Activist, Journalist (1914-1999)

Al Green - Singer, Minister (1946-)

M. Joyce Elders - Civil Servant, Medical Professional, Doctor (1933-)

Sonny Liston - Boxer (1932-1970)

Scottie Pippen - Basketball Player (1940-)

Scott Joplin - Pianist, Songwriter (1868-1912)

Leroy Eldridge Cleaver - Activist, Writer (1935-1998)

E. Lynn Harris - Author (1955-2009)

Maya Angelou - Poet, Dancer, Actress, Singer (1928-2014)

Bill Clinton - U.S. Governor, U.S. President (1946-)

John Grisham - Writer, Author (1955-)

Douglas McArthur - General (1880-1964)

Helen Gurly Brown - Publisher (1922-2012)

Bear Bryant - Football Coach (1913-1983)

Interesting Information

- William Grant Sill, a Little Rock native, was the first African-American conductor of a major symphony and the first black classical composer in the United States.

- Albert "Al" Hibbler was a lead male vocalist for Duke Ellington's orchestra in the 1940s after leaving his Little Rock home.

- Brown n Serve rolls were invented in Little Rock in the 30's by Myer's Bakery.

- Sam Walton founded his Wal-Mart stores in Bentonville.

- Alma claims to be the Spinach Capital of the World.

- General Douglas McArthur, a soldier and statesman, was born in Little Rock in 1880.
- Hope, Arkansas, is the Watermelon Capital of the World.
- Hope, Arkansas, has produced one U.S. President and two Arkansas governors.
- Arkansas is the location of the first diamond mine in the United States.

*****

I cannot tell you why I enjoyed my visit to Little Rock, but I did. Little Rock is the home of Central High School, a National Historic Site. It was here a controversy over the desegregation of schools occurred in the 1950s. In 1957, President Eisenhower sent federal troops to keep Gov. Orval Faubus from blocking racial integration at Central High School. I encourage you to visit the state capitol building and see the statutes of the Little Rock Nine that were led by Mrs. Daisy Bates.

Then, there is the birthplace of William J. Clinton, the 42nd President of the United States. He was born in Hope, Arkansas. He was elected five times as governor and later served two terms as president (1993-2001). His Presidential library in Little Rock opened in 2004. In the library is a full-scale replica of the Cabinet Room where Clinton and his advisers discussed hundreds of topics. It was inspiring to me to see the statues of the Little Rock Nine at the state capitol building.

CALIFORNIA

31st State / September 9, 1850 / Rank in area sq. miles: 3

Nickname: Golden State

Capital: Sacramento

Most populous cities: Los Angeles, San Diego, San Jose, San Francisco

Attractions: *Queen Mary*, Aquarium of the Pacific, in Long Beach; Palomar Observatory, in Palomar Mountain; Disneyland Resort, in Anaheim; Getty Center, Universal Studios Hollywood, Griffith

Observatory, in Los Angeles; Tournament of Roses, in Pasadena; The California Museum, California State Railroad Museum, in Sacramento; San Diego Zoo, USS Midway Museum, in San Diego; Yosemite Valley; Lassen Volcanic, Sequoia, Kings Canyon National Park; Mojave and Sonoran Deserts; Death Valley; Golden Gate Park, Alcatraz Island, in San Francisco, Napa Valley wine region; Monterey Bay Aquarium, Monterey Peninsula; Ancient Bristlecone Pine Forest (oldest known living trees on Earth), in Inyo National Forest; Redwood National and State Parks; Muir Woods National Monument, Mill Valley

Things to see and places to visit in the most populous cities:

Los Angeles - Hollywood, Beverly Hills, Universal Studios, Los Angeles City Hall, Observation Deck at City Hall, Cathedral of Our Lady of the Angeles, Chinatown, Japanese America National Museum, Staple Center, California African American

Museum*, Los Angeles Fashion District, Ralph Bunche House*, Museum of African American Art*

San Diego - Balboa Park, SeaWorld, San Diego Zoo, Gaslamp Quarter, Seaport Village, Point Loma and Cabrillo National Monument, Midway Aircraft Carrier Museum, Horton Plaza

San Jose - Lick Observatory on Mt. Hamilton, Winchester Mystery House, Children's Discovery Museum, Rosicrucian Egyptian Museum, Municipal Rose Garden, Heritage Rose Garden, Tech Museum of Innovation, San Jose State University, San Jose Basilica

San Francisco - Palace of Fine Arts, San Francisco's Chinatown, Alamo Square, Transamerica Pyramid, Lombard Street, Golden Gate Park, Golden Gate Bridge, Alcatraz, Fisherman's Wharf, Cable Cars

Well-known Californians and residents:

Venus Williams - Tennis Player, Athlete (1980-)

Ava DuVernay - Screenwriter, Director, Documentarian (1972-)

Florence Joyner - Track and Field Athlete (1959-1998)

Tyra Banks - Talk Show Host, Model (1973-)

Tiger Woods - Golfer (1975-)

John Singleton - Director, Producer, Screenwriter (1968-)

Darryl Strawberry - Baseball Player (1962-)

D.L. Hughley - Television Actor, Comedian (1963-)

Paul Whitfield - Film Actor, Theater Actor, Television Actor (1941-2004)

Danny Glover - Film Actor (1946-)

Natalie Cole - Singer (1950- 2015)

George Patton - General (1885-1945)

Robert Frost - Educator, Poet (1874-1963)

Angelina Jolie - Film Actress, Director (1975-)

Dianne Feinstein - Mayor, U.S. Representative (1933-)

Ted Danson - Environmental Activist, Film Actor, Television Actor (1947-)

Dave Brubeck - Pianist, Songwriter (1920-2012)

Earl Warren - Governor, Supreme Court Justice (1891-1974)

Jack Kemp - U.S. Representative, Football Player (1935-2009)

Nancy Pelosi - U.S. Representative (1940-)

John Steinbeck - Author (1902-1968)

Ted Williams - Baseball Player, Coach (1918-2002)

Tom Hanks - Film Actor, Television Actor (1956-)

Steve Jobs - Inventor (1955-2011)

Interesting Information

- Only two states, Alaska and Texas, are bigger than California.
- Today, California has the most people than any other state in the U.S.

- One out of every eight United States residents lives in California.
- California has the largest economy of the states in the union. If it were a country, it would have the eighth largest economy in the world, beating out Italy, Russia, and India.
- The United Nations was founded in San Francisco in 1945.
- America's only mobile monument is the cable car in San Francisco.
- California's Mount Whitney measures as the highest peak (14,495 ft.) in the lower 48 states.
- More turkeys are raised in California than in any other state.
- Totaling nearly three million acres, San Bernardino County is the largest county in the country.
- The Hollywood Bowl is the world's largest outdoor amphitheater.

- Death Valley is recognized as the hottest, driest place in the United States. It is not uncommon for the summer temperature to reach more than 115 degrees.
- The first motion picture theater opened in Los Angeles in 1902.
- Fresno proclaims itself the Raisin Capital of the World.

*****

Along with Florida and the mountainous state of Colorado, California is one my favorite. I have traveled from San Diego to the Redwood National Park. There are many attractions in the state, so I say pick your sites to visit for enjoyment. In July 2015, mine was roaming around the University of California, Berkeley, with two of my cousins. In Silicon Valley, we also visited the campuses of Apple (Cupertino), Google (Mt. View) and Facebook (Menlo Park). Let me say that UC Berkeley is one of thirty-one Public Ivy institutions, according to the *University Review*. Public Ivy

32

schools are considered to offer an education at the same level as Ivy League institutions. Following UC Berkeley, some of the institutions are UCLA, University of Michigan, UC at San Diego, University of Wisconsin at Madison, University of Washington at Seattle, University of Illinois at Urbana-Champaign, The University of Texas at Austin, University of Maryland, Pennsylvania State University, UC at Davis, University of North Carolina at Chapel Hill, University of Virginia, University of Florida, and the University of Georgia.

Then I found the Rose Garden in San Jose to be beautiful. I love the stunning beauty of the 17-mile drive along the Pebble Beach and the Monterey Peninsula. I like Palo Alto and the beautiful campus of Stanford University, which must be among one of the most beautiful universities in America. If you visit Stanford, be sure to visit the museum and see *The Thinker* sculpture by Auguste Rodin.

While there are many beautiful cities in America, San Francisco is my favorite. There is something about the Cable Car, Pier 7, the Embarcadero, Pier 39, and many other attractions that fascinate me, as well as walking the streets of San Francisco. The iconic Golden Gate Bridge, was opened in 1937 after five years of construction, is unparalleled. On opening day, around 200,000 bridge walkers marveled at the 4,200-foot-long suspension bridge. On one visit, we crossed the Golden Gate Bridge twice in the same day. San Francisco's skyline is another one of my favorites. Herb Caen said the following about San Francisco: "One day if I go to heaven, I'll look around and say, 'It ain't bad, but it ain't San Francisco." Yes, there was a time when I left my heart in San Francisco.

COLORADO

38th State / August 1, 1876 /rank in area sq. miles: 8

Nickname: The Centennial State

Capital: Denver

Most populous cities: Denver, Colorado Springs,

Aurora

Attractions: Denver Museum of Nature and Science, Denver Botanic Gardens, Denver Zoo, Red Rocks Park and Amphitheater, Morrison, National Center for Atmospheric Research, Boulder; Rocky

Mountain, Black Canyon of the Gunnison, and Mesa Verde (Anasazi cliff dwellings) National Parks; Aspen, Breckenridge, Steamboat, and Vail ski resorts; Garden of the Gods, in Colorado Springs; Great Sand Dunes National Park and Preserve; Dinosaur and Colorado National Monuments; Pikes Peak and Mount Evans; Grand Mesa National Forest; historic mining towns of Central City, Silverton, Cripple Creek; Bent's Old Fort National Historic Site, near La Junta; Georgetown Loop Historic Mining and Railroad Park; Durango and Silverton Narrow Gauge Railroad Museum, Durango; Cumbres and Toltec Scenic Railroad; Black American West Museum and Heritage Center*, in Denver

Things to see and places to visit in the most populous cities:

Denver - Denver Art Museum, Denver Museum of Nature and Science, State Capitol Building, Kirkland Museum of Fine and Decorative Art, Coors

Field, United States Mint, Justina Ford House*, Black American West Museum and Heritage Center*

Colorado Springs - Garden of the Gods, Pikes Peak, Air Force Academy, Ghost Town and Wild West Museum, America the Beautiful Park, Colorado Springs Pioneer Museum, U.S. Olympic Complex Training Center, American Numismatic Association Money Museum

Aurora - Aurora History Museum, Wings Over the Rockies Air and Space Museum

Well-known Coloradans and residents:

Larry Dunn - Music Producer, Pianist, Songwriter (1953-)

Philip Bailey - Singer, Music Producer, Songwriter (1951-)

John Kerry - U.S. Secretary of State, U.S. Representative (1943-)

Tim Allen - Film Actor, Television Actor, Comedian (1953-)

Jack Dempsey - Boxer (1895-1983)

Interesting Information

- More than a 1,000 mountains in Colorado are over 10,000 ft. It is the most mountainous state in the United States.

- Denver lays claim to the invention of the cheeseburger.

- The highest paved road in North America is the road to Mt. Evans off I-70 from Idaho Springs. The road climbs up to 14,258 feet above sea level.

- The United States federal government owns more than 1/3 of the land in Colorado.

- Colorado contains 75% of the land area of the United States with an altitude over 10,000 feet.

- Colfax Avenue in Denver is the longest continuous street in the U.S.

- Katherine Lee Bates wrote "America the Beautiful" after being inspired by the view from Pikes Peak.

- Every year Denver hosts the world's largest rodeo, the Western Stock Show.

- Each year over 400,000 people ascend Pikes Peak, which is 14,110 feet above sea level.

- Colorado's southwest corner borders Arizona, New Mexico, and Utah, the only place in America where corners of four states meet.

*****

Many mountains are in Colorado. Therefore, if you want to get a high other than through legal marijuana sold in the state, then Colorado is the place for you. There are fifty-five mountains over 14,000 feet - Mt. Elbert is the tallest at 14,433 feet.

Colorado offers more mountains above 14,000 feet than any other U. S. state, including Alaska.

For exercise, you may want to walk to the 13th step of the state capitol building in Denver. You will be exactly one mile high above sea level, which is why Denver is called the Mile High City. The U.S. Olympics Training Center and Air Force Academy are in Colorado Springs. The Cadet Chapel at Air Force Academy has amazing beauty. The most striking aspect of the chapel is its row of seventeen spires. Because of its mountains, Colorado is one of my favorite states.

CONNECTICUT

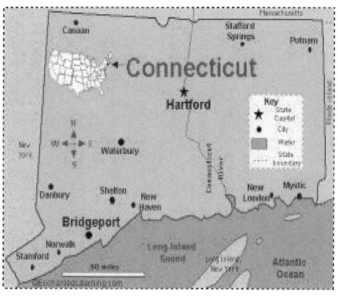

5th State / January 9, 1788 / Rank in area sq. miles:
48

Nickname: The Constitution State,
The Nutmeg State

Capital: Hartford

Most populous cities: Bridgeport, New Haven,
Stamford

Attractions: Mark Twain House and Museum, in Hartford; Yale University Art Gallery, Peabody Museum of Natural History, in New Haven; Mystic

Seaport, Mystic Aquarium, Barnum Museum, in Bridgeport; Gillette Castle State Park, East Haddam; *USS Nautilus* (1st nuclear-powered submarine) at Submarine Force Library and Museum, in Groton; Mashantucker Peqot Museum and Research Center; Philip Johnson Glass House, in New Canaan

Things to see and places to visit in the most populous cities:

Bridgeport - Housatonic Museum of Art, Webster Bank Arena, Discovery Museum, Barnum Museum

New Haven - Yale University, Peabody Museum of Natural History at Yale University, Yale University Art Gallery, The Green

Well-known Connecticutans and residents:

Adam Clayton Powell, Jr. - Civil Rights Activist, Pastor, U.S. Representative (1908-1972)

Constance Baker Motley - Government Official, Lawyer, Judge, Civil Rights Activist (1921-1972)

Edward Alexander Bouchet - Educator (1852-1918)

Harriet Beecher Stowe - Author, Philanthropist (1811-1896)

J. P. Morgan - Business Leader, Art Collector, Philanthropist (1837-1913)

Benedict Arnold - General (1741-1801)

Michael Bolton - Singer (1953-)

Noah Webster - Academic, Journalist (1758-1843)

Benjamin Spock - Medical Professional, Journalist (1903-1998)

Ralph Nader - Environmental Activist, Anti-War Activist (1934-)

Norman Lear - Pilot, Television Producer, Screenwriter (1922-)

John Brown - Civil Rights Activist (1800-1859)

Interesting Information

- The first telephone book issued with 50 names was published in New Haven.
- Connecticut is the home of the oldest U.S. newspaper - the *Hartford Courant*, established in 1764.
- In 1898 the first car insurance in America is issued in Hartford.
- The first cookbook written by an American was published in Hartford in 1796. The book was *American Cookery* by Amelia Simmons.
- Connecticut is home to the first hamburger (1895), helicopter (1939), and color television (1950).

*****

One can find a number of reasons to visit Connecticut, but my first visit was because I wanted to see Yale University, the third oldest university in the country. I remember how I was in awe about the beauty of the campus and Yale on The Green. The

Yale Daily News is the oldest collegiate daily newspaper still in existence.

Five U.S. presidents attended Yale: William Howard Taft, Gerald Ford, George H.W. Bush, William Clinton, and George W. Bush. Ten U.S. presidents who never graduated from college were Andrew Johnson (1865-1869), Zachary Taylor (1849-1850), Millard Fillmore (1850-1853), James Monroe (1817-1825), Andrew Jackson (1829-1837), Grover Cleveland (1885-1889 and 1893-1897), William Henry Harrison (1841), George Washington (1789-1797), Abraham Lincoln (1861-1865), and Harry S. Truman (1945-1953).

The Harriet Beecher Stowe Center is in Hartford. She wrote the anti-slavery novel, *Uncle Tom's Cabin,* in 1852. The Mark Twain House and Museum in Hartford was the home of Samuel Langhorne Clemens (a.k.a. Mark Twain), from 1874-1891 in Hartford. Some of his major works include *The Adventures of Tom Sawyer, Life on the*

Mississippi, and *The Adventures of Huckleberry Finn.*

I still remember visiting the campus of Yale University the summer following my freshman studies. It was one of many colleges and universities I did not know existed when I was growing up in the Florida panhandle.

DELAWARE

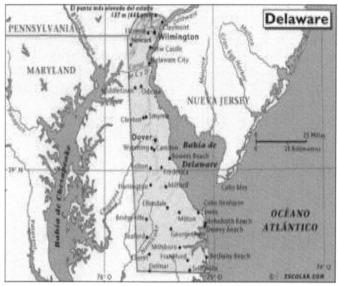

1st State / December 7, 1787 / Rank in area sq. miles: 49

Nickname: First State, Diamond State

Capital: Dover

Most populous cities: Wilmington, Dover, Newark

Attractions: Fort Christina (founding site of New Sweden colony), Holy Trinity (Old Swedes) Church (erected in 1698, oldest church in U.S. still standing as built and in use), Hagley Museum and Library, Nemours Mansion and Gardens, in Wilmington; Winterthur Museum, Garden, and Library, near

47

Wilmington; New Castle Historic District; First State Heritage Park, International Speedway, Richard Allen Marker*, in Dover; Rehoboth Beach

Things to see and places to visit in the most populous cities:

Wilmington - Nemours, Delaware Museum of Natural History, Riverwalk, Delaware State House, Wilmington Race Tracks and Speedways, Wilmington and Western Railroad

Dover - Dover International Speedway, Johnson Victrola Museum, Old State House, Delaware Agricultural Museum and Village, Delaware State Police Museum and Education Center, Delaware State University*, Richard Allen Marker*

Newark - University of Delaware, 9/11 Ribbon Garden at the University of Delaware

Well-known Delawareans and residents:

Clifford Brown - Trumpet Player, Songwriter (1930-1956)

Stephen Marley - Singer, Guitarist (1972-)

John P. Marquand - Author (1893-1960)

Valerie Bertinelli - Film Actress, Television Actress, Journalist (1960-)

E.I. du Pont - Chemist, Scientist (1771-1834)

Joseph Biden - U.S. Vice President, U.S. Senator (1942-)

Interesting Information

- Delaware is the first state in the U.S. because it was the first to accept the Constitution. Delaware is very small, and only Rhode Island has less land.

- Delaware's laws are good for business. That is why many companies have their home offices there.

- The first bathing beauty pageant in which contestants competed for the title of "Miss

United States" took place in Rehoboth Beach in 1880. Inventor Thomas Edison was one of the contest's judges.

*****

Delaware is a mecca for history buffs. The first to ratify the Constitution, it boasts significant sites. A marker in honor of Richard Allen, founder of the African Methodist Church, is in Dover. Allen purchased his freedom and went to Philadelphia, where he played a leading role in both the religious and political history of black Americans in the early nineteenth century.

Woodburn, the Dover governor's mansion since 1965, was reputed to have been a station on the Underground Railroad.

FLORIDA

27th State / March 3, 1845 / Rank in area sq. miles: 22

Nickname: Sunshine State

Capital: Tallahassee

Most populous cities: Jacksonville, Miami, Tampa, St. Petersburg, Orlando

Attractions: Miami Beach; Castillo de San Marcos National Monument, St. Augustine Lighthouse and Museum, Lightner Museum, in St. Augustine (oldest permanent European settlement in the U.S.); Walt

Disney World Resort, SeaWorld Orlando, Universal Studios, Discovery Cove, in Orlando; Kennedy Space Center, U.S. Astronaut Hall of Fame; Everglades National Park; Ringling Museum of Art, Ringling Circus Museum, in Sarasota; Cypress Gardens at Legoland Florida, in Winter Haven; Busch Gardens, Big Cat Rescue, in Tampa; Florida Caverns State Park, in Marianna; Key West, Mary McLeod Bethune House,* Bethune-Cookman University campus,* and Howard Thurman House*, in Daytona Beach; Meek-Eaton Southeastern Regional Black Archives, Florida A&M University*, in Tallahassee; Zora Neale Hurston House*, in Fort Pierce

Things to see and places to visit in the most populous cities:

Jacksonville - The Beach, Jacksonville's Riverside District, Jacksonville Landing, Jacksonville Zoo and Gardens, Everbank Field, Friendship Fountain, Edwin M. Stanton School*, where James Weldon Johnson was a student and served as principal from

52

1894 to 1902, Centennial Hall - Edward Waters College*

Miami - South Beach, Everglades, Zoo Miami, Seaquarium, Miami Beach, Ocean Drive, Bayfront Park, Little Havana and Calle Ocho, American Airlines Arena, Gold Coast Railroad Museum

Tampa - Busch Gardens, Ybor City, Sunshine Skyway, Bayshore Boulevard, Florida Aquarium, Sergengeti Night Safari at Busch Gardens, Raymond James Stadium, Museum of African American Art*

St. Petersburg - The Dali Museum, Sunken Gardens

Orlando - Walt Disney World, Seaworld, Universal Studios, Discovery Cove, Typhoon Lagoon, Islands of Adventure, Wet 'N' Wild, Orlando Science Center, Gatorland, Holy Land Experience, Ripley's Believe It Or Not Orlando, Epcot, Magic Kingdom, Orlando Museum of Art - African Gallery*

Well-known Floridians and residents:

A. Philip Randolph - Civil Rights Activist (1899-1979)

Wally Amos - Entrepreneur (1936-)

Sidney Poitier - Film Actor, Filmmaker (1927-)

David "Deacon" Jones - Football Player, Athlete (1938-2013)

Ben Vereen - Actor (1946-)

James Weldon Johnson - Diplomat, Educator, Civil Rights Activist, Literary Critic, Songwriter, Lawyer, Poet, Author (1871-1938)

Daniel James, Jr. - General, Pilot (1920-1978)

Deion Sanders - Baseball Player, Football Player (1967-)

Ester Rolle - Film Actress, Theater Actress, Television Actress (1920-1998)

Bob Hayes - Football Player, Track and Field Athlete (1942-2002)

Augusta Savage - Sculptor, Artist, Educator, Civil Rights Activist (1892-1962)

Emmitt Smith - Football Player (1969-)

Bob Villa - Entrepreneur, Television Host
(1946-)

Faye Dunaway - Film Actress, Theater Actress,
Television Actress (1941-)

Chris Evert - Tennis Player, Athlete (1954-)

Bubba Watson - Golfer (1978-)

Claude Pepper - U.S. Senator, U.S.
Representative (1900-1989)

Janet Reno - U.S. Attorney General (1938-2016)

Interesting Information

- Florida means "Feast of Flowers" in Spanish.

- The state has the second longest coastline in
  the U.S.

- Florida has 663 miles of beaches and 1,800
  miles of coastline.

- The Everglades is one of the largest swamps
  in the world.

- Dr. John Gorrie of Apalachicola invented
  mechanical refrigeration in 1851.

- Florida produces 75% of the U.S. oranges.

- The longest river is the St. Johns at 273 miles.

- Palm Beach County has more golf courses than any other county in the country.

- Florida's capitol is a 22-story building with three floors underground.

- Saint Augustine is the oldest European settlement in North America.

- Orlando attracts more visitors than any other amusement park destinations in the United States.

- St. John's River is one of the few rivers that flows north instead of south.

- Ft. Lauderdale is known as the Venice of America because the city has 185 miles of local waterways.

- Florida is the only state that has 2 rivers with the same name. There is a Withlacoochee in north central Florida (Madison County) and a Withlacoochee in central Florida. They have nothing in common except the name.

- The largest collection of Frank Lloyd Wright buildings in the world is in Lakeland.
- The phrase "cool as a cucumber" originated in Florida.
- No matter where you are in Florida you are never more than 60 miles from the ocean.
- It takes 62,000 people to create the *Magic* at the Vacation Kingdom.
- Magic Kingdom ranks as the third most popular tourist attraction in the world.
- Florida is the most populous state, after California, Texas and New York.

*****

Florida's landmass is basically a large peninsula with the Gulf of Mexico to the west and the Atlantic Ocean to the east. It is the fourth most populous state in the United States and spans 792 miles from Key West to Pensacola. On one tour we traveled from one end of the state to the other.

Saint Augustine, the oldest European settlement in North America is, along with Walt Disney World, the most popular tourist attraction on the planet. Florida has miles and miles of beaches; some have sand so white it looks sugary. Two of my favorites on the Atlantic Ocean are Daytona Beach and Clearwater Beach, and on the Gulf, Mexico Beach in Port St. Joe (it is quiet and serene) and Destin for its beauty.

When I am asked about well-known Floridians, the one I mention the most is James Weldon Johnson. He was a diplomat, educator, civil rights activist, literary critic, songwriter, lawyer, poet, and an author. His mother was the first black teacher in Florida and taught at Stanton School in Jacksonville. Johnson attended Stanton until he left to attend Atlanta University; he later returned as principal. He wrote the words to the poem "Lift Every Voice and Sing." It was written in part as celebration of Abraham Lincoln's birthday February 12, 1900. The poem was set to music in 1905 by his brother Rosemond. It was dubbed the National Negro Anthem by the NAACP in 1919. A James Weldon Johnson marker is at the Edwin M. Stanton School, 521 Ashley Street, in Jacksonville.

The Meek-Eaton Black Archives Research Center and Museum is in the Carnegie Library on the Campus of Florida A&M University, my alma mater, in Tallahassee. It focuses on African-American history in Florida. Included are contributions of the African-American church, important figures in politics, science, medicine, inventors, military experience and more. It is on the U. S. Register of National Historic Places.

Also, Bethune Cookman University, founded by Dr. Mary McLeod Bethune in 1904, is located in Daytona Beach. Dr. Bethune was an educator, an administrator, a presidential adviser, and a civil rights leader. She was born in a wooden cabin near Mayesville, South Carolina, the fifteenth child of parents who were slaves. Her home is on campus and is open for tours. She died in 1955 at the age of eighty and is buried on campus.

Lastly, built in 1916, Centennial Hall is the oldest building on the campus of Edward Waters College in Jacksonville. The building was named to commemorate the 100th anniversary of the African Methodist Episcopal (AME) Church. The school was renamed Edward Waters College, after the third bishop of the AME Church. It was at Edward Waters College, where I was taught by Dr. Leonard F. Morse, Sr. He and two other daring students founded Phi Beta Sigma Fraternity, Inc., at Howard University in 1914.

GEORGIA

4th State / January 2, 1788 / Rank in area sq. miles: 24

Nickname: Empire State of the South, Peach State

Capital: Atlanta

Most populous cities: Atlanta, Augusta, Columbus, Savannah

Attractions: Georgia State Capitol, Stone Mountain, Centennial Olympic Park, Six Flags Over Georgia,

Martin Luther King, Jr. National Historic Site*, Jimmy Carter Library and Museum, Atlanta Botanical Garden, Georgia Aquarium (world's largest), in Atlanta; Kennesaw Mountain National Battlefield Park; Chickamauga and Chattanooga National Military Park; Chattahoochee-Oconee National Forest; Dahlonega, site of earliest U.S. gold rush; Brass-White House Historic Site, in Warm Springs; Callaway Gardens, in Pine Mountain; Andersonville National Historic Site (Confederate military prison); Okefenokee National Wildlife Refuge; Jekyll, St. Simons, and Cumberland barrier islands; Savannah Historic District, First African Baptist Church*, in Savannah; The Tubman African American Museum*, in Macon; Albany Civil Rights Institute*; Columbus Black History Museum and Archives*

Things to see and places to visit in the most populous cities:

Atlanta - Martin Luther King, Jr. National Historic Site*, Atlanta History Center, Fox Theater, World of Coca-Cola, Fernbank Museum of Natural History, Georgia Aquarium, Ebenezer Baptist Church of Atlanta*, Jimmy Carter Library and Museum, College Football Hall of Fame, CNN Studio Tour, Center for Civil and Human Rights, Atlanta University Center District*; Sweet Auburn Historic District*; Martin Luther King, Jr. Birthplace*; The Center for Civil and Human Rights*; APEX Museum*

Augusta - Augusta Riverwalk, Boyhood Home of Woodrow Wilson, The Signers Monument, The Lucy Craft Laney Museum of Black History*

Columbus - Columbus Museum, National Infantry Museum

Savannah - River Street, Mrs. Wilkes Boarding House, Juliette Low House, Bull Street, Squares of Savannah, Riverfront, Cathedral of St. John the Baptist, First African Baptist Church*

Well-known Georgians and residents:

Martin Luther King, Jr. - Civil Rights Activist, Minister (1929-1968)

Jackie Robinson - Baseball Player (1919-1972)

Otis Redding - Singer, Songwriter (1941-1967)

Ray Charles - Singer, Pianist, Songwriter (1930-2004)

Alice Walker - Women's Rights Activist, Author, Civil Rights Activist (1944-)

Wayne Brady - Game Show Host, Talk Show Host, Television Actor, Comedian (1972-)

Nipsey Russell - Actor, Comedian (1924-2005)

Gladys Knight - Film Actress, Singer, Songwriter (1944-)

Joe Williams - Singer (1918-1999)

Walter White - Civil Rights Activist, Author, Journalist (1893-1955)

Jessye Norman - Singer (1945-)

Spike Lee - Film Actor, Director, Producer (1957-)

Vernon Jordan - Business Leader, Civil Rights Activist, Lawyer (1935-)

Ossie Davis - Civil Rights Activist, Actor, Director, Playwright (1917-2005)

LeRoy Walker - Coach (1918-2012)

Elijah Muhammad - Religious Figure (1897-1975)

Pinckney Pinchback - Civil Rights Activist, U.S. Representative, U.S. Governor (1837-1921)

Ben Bernanke - Economist (1953-)

Harry James - Trumpet Player, Conductor, Songwriter (1916-1983)

Brenda Lee - Singer (1944-)

Juliette Gordon Low - Philanthropist (1860-1927)

Julia Roberts - Film Actress, Television Producer (1967-)

Jimmy Carter - U.S. President (1924-)

Pat Conroy - Educator, Author, Journalist (1945-2016)

Interesting Information

- Georgia is the largest state east of the Mississippi River.

- Atlanta is the home of CNN and Coca-Cola.

- The world's largest military infantry training center is located at Ft. Benning.

- The largest Farmer's Market of its kind is located in Forest Park.

- Historic Saint Mary's, Georgia, is the second oldest city in the nation.

- First African Baptist Church in Savannah is the oldest Black church in North America. It was constituted in 1777.

- Just outside of Atlanta, the community of Serenbe requires each of its 200-plus homes to include a porch.

*****

If you have Georgia on your mind, Atlanta is the home of Coca-Cola, Delta Airlines, Home Depot, Turner Broadcasting and the United Postal Service. If presidential libraries - there are thirteen to date - are on your list of places to visit, the Jimmy Carter Presidential Library is in Atlanta. Carter is one of only four presidents to win the Nobel Prize (the others are Theodore Roosevelt, Woodrow Wilson and Barack Obama).

One of Georgia's most well-known natives is Dr. Martin Luther King, Jr., whose birth home and National Historic Site are in Atlanta. A visit to the Atlanta University District, Morehouse College, the MLK Jr. International Chapel, and the International Hall of Honor will give you a feeling of awe and inspiration.

Savannah, one of the top city destinations in the U.S., has a lot of history. Girl Scout founder Juliette Gordon Low was born in Savannah. With its twenty-two park-like squares, it is one of the largest Historic Landmark Districts in the United States. One of the oldest African-American churches in North America, the First African Baptist Church, is in Savannah. The church's archives room with ledgers displaying disputes and differences between officers and/or members will both surprise and amuse you.

We often hear about going down memory lane. Well, for me a ride down beautiful Victory Drive in Savannah is akin to being on memory lane.

Augusta has The Lucy Craft Laney Museum of Black History. The mission is to promote the legacy of Miss Lucy Craft Laney through art, history, and the presentation of her home. Macon has the Harriet Tubman Museum. Its mission is to educate people about art, history, and culture of African Americans. A significant event occurred on April 20, 2016, the day the U.S. Treasury Department announced a plan for Harriet Tubman to replace Andrew Jackson as the portrait gracing the $20 bill. I was actually visiting the museum with a friend when the announcement was made, and we were interviewed by a reporter from the *Macon Telegraph*.

HAWAII

50th State / August 21, 1959 / Rank in area sq. miles: 43

Nickname: Aloha State

Capital: Honolulu

Most populous cities: Honolulu, Hilo, Kailua

Attractions: Oahu Island; Oahu Island National Memorial Cemetery of the Pacific, Waikiki Beach, Diamond Head, in Honolulu; *USS Arizona* Memorial, Pearl Harbor; Polynesian Cultural Center,

70

in Laie; Hanauma Bay; Nu'uanu Pali, Kaua'I Island; Waimea Canyon, Maui Island; Haleakala National Park, Hawaii Island; Volcanoes National Park, Wailoa and Wailuku River state parks

Things to see and places to visit in the most populous cities:

Honolulu - Pearl Harbor and *USS Arizona* Memorial, Waikiki, Iolani Palace, Bishop Museum and Planetarium, Honolulu Chinatown, Diamond Head, Honolulu Zoo/Waikiki Aquarium, Honolulu Fish Auction

Hilo - The rain (the rainiest city in the U.S.), the Orchids, the farmer's market, the beach

Kailua - The Beach, Kailua Beach, Lanika Beach, instant waterfalls in the cliffs

Well-known Hawaiians and residents:

Barack H. Obama - Lawyer, U.S. Representative, U.S. President (1961-)

Bette Midler - Actress, Singer, Comedian (1945-)

Nicole Kidman - Film Actress (1967-)

Don Ho - Singer (1930-2007)

Michelle Wie - Golfer, Athlete (1989-)

Liliuokalani - Queen (1838-1917)

Interesting Information

- Hawaii is the only state made up of islands. It has 132 islands, stretching over 1,500 miles in the Pacific Ocean. The Island of Hawaii is the biggest. It is the most southern place in the U.S.

- Hawaii is the most isolated populated center on the face of the earth.

- Hawaii is 2,390 miles from California; 3,850 miles from Japan; 4,900 miles from China; and 5,280 miles from the Philippines.

- From east to west Hawaii is the widest state in the United States.

- Hawaii is the only state that grows coffee.

- More than 100 world-renowned beaches are in Honolulu.

- Kilauea volcano is the world's most active.
- Mauna Kea is the tallest mountain in the world (measured from its base at the ocean floor).
- Iolani Palace is the only royal palace in the United States.
- Hawaii is the only state covered entirely by its own time zone, Hawaii-Aluetian, and it also does not observe daylight saving time.

*****

Hawaii has a vast number of natural, cultural and historical attractions from which you can choose. Two of the major attractions are Waikiki Beach and Pearl Harbor *USS Arizona* Memorial. Maui is known for its miles of stunning beaches and luxurious hideaways.

One unique aspect of Hawaii's demography is that no one ethnic group makes up a majority of the state's population. Over a third of the island's residents are of mixed races.

IDAHO

43rd State / July 3, 1890 / Rank in area
sq. miles: 14

Nickname: Gem State

Capital: Boise

Most populous cities: Boise, Nampa, Meridian

Attractions: Hells Canyon (deepest river gorge in North America), Boise Art Museum, in Boise; Craters of the Moon National Monument and

Preserve; Sun Valley; Shoshone Falls, near Twin Falls; Lake Coeur d'Alene

Things to see and places to visit in the most populous cities:

Boise - State Capitol, Idaho Anne Frank Human Rights Memorial, Idaho Botanical Gardens, Discovery Center of Idaho, Basque Museum and Cultural Center, Christ Chapel at Boise State University, Boise Train Depot

Nampa - Northwest Nazarene University, Canyon County Historical Museum

Meridian - Dart Zone Meridian

Well-known Idahoans and residents:

Ezra Pound - Poet, Journalist (1885-1972)
Lana Turner - Actress, Pin-Up (1921-1995)
Picabo Street - Athlete (1971-)

Interesting Information

- Hells Canyon is the deepest gorge in America (7,900 ft. deep).

- Rexburg is home to Ricks College, the largest private two-year college in the nation.

- The statehouse in Boise is geothermally heated from underground hot springs.

- Idaho has 3,100 miles of rivers - more than any other state.

- Idaho is the number one producer of potatoes.

*****

Idaho is known as the Potato State. It is one of the most sparsely populated states in the U.S. People outside of Idaho eat more potatoes than people in Idaho. Downtown Boise is 2,704 feet above sea level. The Boise State University Broncos play on the world's only blue football field, known as The Smurf Turf.

ILLINOIS

21ˢᵗ State / December 3, 1818 / Rank in area sq. miles: 25

Nickname: Prairie State, Land of Lincoln

Capital: Springfield

Most populous cities: Chicago, Aurora, Rockford

Attractions: Field Museum of Natural History, Shedd Aquarium, Millennium Park, Navy Pier, in Chicago; Illinois State Museum, Abraham Lincoln

Presidential Library and Museum, Lincoln Home National Historic Site, Lincoln's Tomb State Historic Site, in Springfield; Du Sable Museum of African-American History*, Harold Washington Library Center*, Ida B. Wells-Barnett House*, Oscar Stanton DePriest House*, Dr. Daniel Hale Williams House*, in Chicago

Things to see and places to visit in the most populous cities:

Chicago - Art Institute of Chicago, Millennium Park, Michigan Avenue and the Magnificent Mile, Navy Pier, Wrigley Field, Museum of Science and Industry, Field Museum of Natural History, Willis Tower SkyDeck, Garfield Park Conservatory, John Hancock Center

Aurora - Aurora Regional Fire Museum, Tanner House Museum, Blackberry Farm

Rockford - Burpee Museum of Natural History, Anderson Japanese Gardens

Well-known Illinoisans and residents:

Common - Film Actor, Rapper, Songwriter, Television Actor (1972-)

Patricia Roberts Harris - Government Official (1924-1985)

Miles Davis - Trumpet Player, Songwriter (1926-1991)

Shonda Rhimes - Television Producer, Screenwriter (1970-)

Richard Pryor - Actor, Comedian, Screenwriter (1940-2005)

Michelle Obama - U.S. First Lady, Lawyer (1964-)

Deval Patrick - Legal Professional, Governor (1956-)

Curtis Mayfield - Singer (1942-1999)

Harold Washington - Mayor, U.S. Representative (1922-1987)

Quincy Jones - Children's Activist, Trumpet Player, Music Producer, Songwriter, Television Producer (1933-)

Lorraine Hansberry - Playwright (1930-1965)

Don Cornelius - Television Personality, Television Producer (1936-2012)

Bernard Shaw - News Anchor, Journalist (1940-)

Jane Addams - Women's Rights Activist, Anti-War Activist, Philanthropist (1860-1935)

Ethel Kennedy - Human Rights Campaigner (1928-)

Betty White - Television Actress, Animal Rights Activist, Comedian (1922-)

Walt Disney - Producer, Entrepreneur (1901-1966)

Hillary Clinton - Government Official, U.S. First Lady, Women's Rights Activist, U. S. Secretary of State (1947-)

Harrison Ford - Film Actor (1942-)

Interesting Information

- The world's first skyscraper was built in Chicago in 1885.

- Des Plaines is the home of the first McDonald's.
- Nabisco, the world's largest cookie and cracker factory, is located in Chicago.
- Chicago's post office at 433 Van Buren is the only postal facility in the world you can drive a car through.
- The first Aquarium opened in Chicago in 1885.
- The Chicago Public Library is the world's largest with a collection of more than 2 million books.
- Illinois is home to the world's largest bottle of catsup.
- Aurora is known as the City of Lights because it was the first U.S. city to use electric street lighting throughout the entire city.
- The Lincoln Park Zoo in Chicago is one of only three major free zoos in the country, and it is the nation's oldest public zoo.

- The world's tallest man was born in Alton, IL. Robert Pershing Wadlow was 8'11", weighed 491 lbs., and wore a size 37 shoe.
- Nearly 80% of the state's land is farm land.
- Chicago River is the only river in the world that flows backwards.
- The remote control was invented in Chicago in 1950.

*****

Chicago was founded in 1772. Jean-Baptiste Point du Sable, a man from Haiti, established a settlement on the north bank of Chicago River, calling it Eschikagou. The Du Sable Museum of African American History in Chicago is one of the oldest Black history museums.

For those who have traveled the "Historic Route 66" from Chicago to Los Angeles, or vice versa as I have, the Route begins in Chicago at Grant Park on Adams Street in front of the Art Institute of Chicago.

You cannot truly experience Chicago without a ride down Lake Michigan Boulevard or a visit to Navy Pier. The Pier is a playground of entertainment, museums, activities, restaurants, and shops. Chicago has 26 miles of lakefront.

Abraham Lincoln Presidential Library and Museum is in Springfield, the state capital. "A house divided against itself cannot stand …." These immortal words were spoken by Abraham Lincoln in the historic Old State Capitol Hall of Representatives in the turbulent days preceding the Civil War. It was the capitol area where Senator Barack Obama announced he would run for president in 2008.

INDIANA

19th State / December 11, 1816 / Rank in area sq. miles: 38

Nickname: Hoosier State

Capital: Indianapolis

Most populous cities: Indianapolis, Fort Wayne, Evansville

Attractions: Lincoln Boyhood Home National Memorial, in Lincoln City; Tippecanoe Battlefield Museum and Park, in Battleground; Benjamin

Harrison Presidential Site, Indianapolis Motor Speedway and Hall of Fame Museum, Indianapolis Museum of Art, in Indianapolis; College Football Hall of Fame; Studebaker National Museum, in South Bend; Hoosier National Forest; Levi Coffin House

Things to see and places to visit in the most populous cities:

Indianapolis - Indianapolis Museum of Art, Children's Museum of Indianapolis, Indianapolis Speedway, White River State Park, Benjamin Harrison Presidential Site, State Capitol Building, Madam C. J. Walker Urban Life Center*

Fort Wayne - Snite Museum of Art, Indiana University Art Museum

Evansville - Hands On Discovery Children's Museum, Angel Mounds Historic Site

Well-known Indianians and residents:

Noble Sissle - Singer, Songwriter, Playwright (1889-1975)

Vivica A. Fox - Film Actress, Reality Television Star, Television Actress (1964-)

Michael Warren - Television Actor (1946-)

Babyface - Singer, Guitarist, Songwriter, Producer (1959-)

Major Taylor - Cyclist (1878-1932)

Oscar Robertson - Basketball Player (1938-)

Sarah "Madam C.J." Walker - Civil Rights Activist, Philanthropist, Entrepreneur (1867-1919)

Michael Jackson - Singer, Music Producer (1958-2009)

Jane Pauley - Talk Show Host, News Anchor (1950-)

John Wooden - Basketball Player, Coach (1910-2010)

Gus Grissom - Astronaut (1926-1967)

Steve Kroft - News Anchor, Journalist (1945-)

Larry Bird - Basketball Player, Coach (1966-)

Wilbur Wright - Inventor (1867-1912)

David Letterman - Talk Show Host, Comedian (1947-)

Interesting Information

- The first professional baseball game was played in Ft. Wayne on May 4, 1871.

- Indiana has more miles of Interstate highway than any other state. (It is known as the crossroads of America.)

- Wabash, Indiana, was the first city in the United States to have electric streetlights, which came on at 8 p.m. on March 31, 1880.

- Santa Claus, Indiana, receives over one half million letters and requests at Christmas time.

- New Harmony, Indiana, was the first place in the United States where boys and girls were taught in the same classes.

- Abraham Lincoln grew up in Indiana, where he lived on a farm for 14 years.

- Many families in Indiana provided shelter for runaway slaves before and during the Civil War. In particular, the farming community of Newport (now Fountain City) became known as the "Grand Central Station of the Underground Railroad" due to Levi and Catherine Coffin's roles in helping more than 2,000 runaway slaves make their way north to freedom.

*****

Indiana is nicknamed "The Crossroads of America" because of the junction of Interstate highways. Some of the more interesting attractions on my visit were the Indianapolis Motor Speedway, the Indiana State Capitol, and the Monument Circle/Soldiers and Sailors War Memorial. Constructed in 1927, the Walker Building was the site of the successful beauty products' firm of Madam C. J. Walker. The Bethel AME Church in Indianapolis purportedly participated in the

Underground Railroad, aiding escaped slaves in their flight to Canada.

If you go through Gary, then you may want to visit the neighborhood where Michael Jackson and the Jackson family lived. One of Tito Jackson's high school classmates told me tourists visit daily. A month after my visit, I saw Jermaine Jackson in Brussels, Belgium, and got his autograph for my granddaughter.

IOWA

29th State / December 28, 1846 / Rank in
area sq. miles: 26

Nickname: Hawkeye State

Capital: Des Moines

Most populous cities: Des Moines,
Cedar Rapids, Davenport

Attractions: Iowa State Capitol, in Des Moines; Des
Moines Art Center, Herbert Hoover National
Historic Site, Presidential Library and Museum,

in West Branch; Effigy Mounds National Monument, in Marquette; Adventureland, in Altoona; National Mississippi River Museum and Aquarium, in Dubuque

Things to see and places to visit in the most populous cities:

Des Moines - State Capitol (one of the most beautiful capitols in the U.S.), Greater Des Moines Botanical Center, Des Moines Art Center, Science Center of Iowa, Public Library of Des Moines National Bar Association Collection, and Jordan House Museum in West Des Moines

Cedar Rapids - Brucemore, Cedar Rapids Museum of Art, Cedar Rapids Science and Technology Museum

Davenport - Vander Veer Botanical Center and Park, Chocolate Manor

Well-known Iowans and residents:

Tionne "T-Boz" Watkins - Singer (1970-)

Mamie Eisenhower - U.S. First Lady (1896-1979)

Donna Reed - Television Actress (1921-1986)

Ann Landers - Writer (1918-2002)

Johnny Carson - Television Show Host (1925-2005)

Andy Williams - Singer, Television Personality (1927-2012)

Interesting Information

- Strawberry Point is the home of the world's largest strawberry.
- Quaker Oats, Cedar Rapids, is the largest cereal company in the world.
- Dubuque is the home to the only county courthouse with a gold dome.
- Cornell College is the only school in the nation to have its entire campus listed on the National Register of Historic Places.

- Iowa is the only state name that starts with two vowels.
- Iowa State University is the oldest land grant college in the United States.

*****

One of my favorite places to visit in a state is the state capitol. I have seen forty-five out of the fifty capitols. The ones I have not seen are Michigan, Missouri, Montana, New Hampshire, and New York. Of the capitol buildings I have seen, I think Iowa's capitol in Des Moines is the prettiest. The building is beautiful! It is the only five-domed state capitol in the United States and one of the largest in size. It has a 23-karat gold leaf dome. The gardens surrounding the capitol, the memorials on the grounds, and the view of downtown from the west side of the capitol is magnificent.

KANSAS

34th State / January 29, 1861 / Rank in area sq. miles: 15

Nickname: Sunflower State, Jayhawk State

Capital: Topeka

Most populous cities: Wichita, Overland Park, Kansas City

Attractions: Eisenhower Presidential Library and Museum, in Abilene; National Agricultural Center and Hall of Fame, in Bonner Springs; Boot Hill Museum, in Dodge City; Old Cowtown Museum, in Wichita; Ft. Scott and Ft. Larned National Historic

Site; Kansas Cosmosphere and Space Center, in Hutchinson; U.S. Calvary Museum, in Ft. Riley; Kansas City Speedway, in Kansas City; George Washington Carver Homestead Site*, Beeler (Ness County); Brown v. Board of Education National Historic Landmark (Sumner Elementary School and Monroe Elementary School*), in Topeka

Things to see and places to visit in the most populous cities:

Wichita - Exploration Place, Museum of World Treasures, Cowtown, Kansas Sports Hall of Fame, L.D. Holmes Museum of Anthropology - Wichita State University, The Kansas African American Museum*, Wichita Art Museum, Wichita State University

Overland Park - Nerman Museum of Contemporary Art, Museum at Prairiefire, American Museum of Natural History, Overland Park 9/11 Memorial

Kansas City - National World War I Museum at Liberty Memorial, Kemper Museum of Contemporary Art, Union Station, Hallmark Visitors Center, Negro Leagues Baseball Museum*, Science City at Union Station

Well-known Kansans and residents:

Hattie McDaniel - Film Actress (1895-1952)

Gale Sayers - Football Player, Athlete (1943-)

Charlie Parker - Saxophonist, Songwriter (1920-1955)

Linda Brown - Civil Rights Activist (1942-)

Gwendolyn Brooks - Poet (1917-2000)

Gordon Parks - Writer, Photographer, Pianist, Songwriter, Director (1912-2006)

Annette Bening - Film Actress (1958-)

Amelia Earhart - Pilot (1897-1939)

Vivian Vance - Film Actress, Television Actress (1909-1979)

Dennis Hopper - Film Actor, Television Actor, Director (1936-2010)

Interesting Information

- Dodge City is the windiest city in the United States.

- The first black woman who received an Academy Award was Kansan Hattie McDaniel. She won the award for her role in *Gone with the Wind*.

- Smith County is the geographical center of the 48 contiguous states.

- The world famous fast-food chain Pizza Hut opened its first store in Wichita.

- Sumner County is known as "The Wheat Capital of the World."

- George Washington Carver, the famous botanical scientist who discovered more than 300 products made from peanuts, graduated from high school in Minneapolis in 1885.

Kansas is referred to as the American "Heartland." Fire Station No. 4 in Lawrence, originally a stone barn constructed in 1858, was a station on the Underground Railroad.

I am one who gets pleasure from visiting presidential libraries. While passing through Abilene on one trip, we visited the Eisenhower Presidential Library and Museum. We also stopped at the Dwight D. and Mamie D. Eisenhower burial site. The Eisenhower Presidential Library and Museum is nearby. The Brown v. Board of Education National Historic Landmark is in Topeka.

If you want to visit Middle America, go to Kansas. It is located almost directly in the center of the continental United States.

KENTUCKY

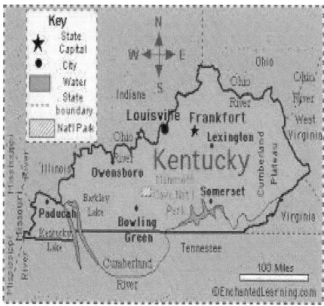

15th State / June 1, 1792 / Rank in area sq. miles: 37

Nickname: Bluegrass State

Capital: Frankfort

Most populous cities: Louisville, Lexington, Bowling Green

Attractions: Churchill Downs (Kentucky Derby), Louisville Slugger Museum and Factory, in Louisville; Mammoth Cave National Park (world's largest known cave system); Abraham Lincoln

Birthplace National Historical Park, in Hodgenville; My Old Kentucky Home State Park, in Bardstown; Cumberland Gap National Historical Park, in Middlesboro; Kentucky Horse Park, in Lexington; National Corvette Museum, in Bowling Green; Whitney M. Young, Jr. Birthplace*, in Simpsonville; Berea College

Things to see and places to visit in the most populous cities:

Louisville - Kentucky Derby, Louisville Slugger Museum, Muhammad Ali Center, Muhammad Ali Childhood Home Museum*, Speed Art Museum, Thomas Edison House, Gallopalooza Horses

Lexington - Kentucky Horse Park, Mary Todd Lincoln House, University of Kentucky Art Museum, Rupp Arena, Thoroughbred Park, Isaac Murphy Memorial*

Bowling Green - National Corvette Museum, Western Kentucky University, Historic Railroad Park and Train Museum, Fountain Square Park

Well-known Kentuckians and residents:

Muhammad Ali - Boxer, Philanthropist (1942-2016)

Countee Cullen - Poet, Playwright, Author (1903-1946)

Whitney M. Young, Jr. - Civil Rights Activist (1921-1971)

Garret Morgan - Inventor, Publisher (1877-1963)

Lionel Hampton - (1908-2002)

Isaac Burns Murphy - Athlete (1861-1896)

Diana Sawyer - News Anchor, Journalist (1945-)

Robert Penn Warren - Civil Rights Activist, Literary Critic, Poet (1905-1989)

John Marshall Harlan - Civil Rights Activist, Lawyer, Supreme Court Justice (1833-1911)

Abraham Lincoln - Civil Rights Activist, Lawyer, U.S. Representative, U.S. President (1809-1865)

Interesting Information

- Cheeseburgers were first served in 1934 at Kaolin's Restaurant in Louisville.
- Chevrolet's Corvettes are manufactured in Bowling Green.
- The first KFC restaurant is located in Corbin.
- The song "Happy Birthday to You" is the creation of two Louisville sisters in 1893.
- Berea College was the first college formed for the purpose of admitting black and white students.

*****

Kentucky is the state where both Abraham Lincoln, President of the Union, and Jefferson Davis, President of the Confederacy, were born. They were born less than one hundred miles apart and one year apart. The state is probably better known for the Kentucky Derby and Churchill Downs held in Louisville the first Saturday in May. Kentucky is the Bluegrass State, but not all of the grass is blue. Some of the grass has a blue tint.

I enjoyed the breathtaking view at Cumberland Falls State Resort Park and the floral clock in Frankfort on the lawn of the state capitol. The word "Kentucky" is spelled out in large letters around the top of the clock.

LOUISIANA

18th State / April 30, 1812 / Rank in area sq. miles:
31

Nickname: Pelican State

Capital: Baton Rouge

Most populous cities: New Orleans, Baton Rouge,
Shreveport

Attractions: Mardi Gras, French Quarter, Bourbon
Street, Louis Armstrong Park, Preservation Hall,

Old Mint Museum, in New Orleans; Gardens State Park, in Florien; USS Kidd Veterans Memorial, in Baton Rouge; Southern University Archives Building*, in Scotlandville; Armistad Research Center at Tulane University; Arna Bontemps African American Museum*, in Alexandria

Things to see and places to visit in the most populous cities:

New Orleans - French Quarter, Mardi Gras, Bourbon Street, Jackson Square, Royal Street, St. Louis Cathedral, Preservation Hall, Mardi Gras World, Steamboat Natchez, National WWII Museum, Armistad Research Center, Louis Armstrong Park*

Baton Rouge - Old State Capitol, USS Kidd and Veterans Memorial, Louisiana State University, Louisiana State Capitol, LSU Rural Life Museum, Louisiana Arts and Science Museum

Shreveport - Shreveport Water Works Museum, Louisiana State Exhibit Museum, Cathedral of St. John Berchmans, Southern University Museum of Art at Shreveport*, Antioch Baptist Church*, Riverview Park

Well-known Louisianans and residents:

Arna Bontemps - Writer, Author (1902-1973)

Madam C. J. Walker - Civil Rights Activist, Philanthropist, Entrepreneur (1867-1919)

Louis Armstrong - Trumpet Player, Singer (1901-1971)

Tyler Perry - Film Actor, Filmmaker, Screenwriter, Playwright (1969-)

Johnnie Cochran - Lawyer (1937-2005)

Andrew Young, Jr. - Diplomat, Educator, Civil Rights Activist, Mayor, Pastor, U.S. Representative (1932-)

Bill Russell - Basketball Player, Coach (1934-)

Wynton Marsalis - Trumpet Player, Songwriter (1961-)

Mahalia Jackson - Singer, Television Personality, Civil Rights Activist (1911-1972)

Evelyn Ashford - Track and Field Athlete (1957-)

Huey Newton - Political Activist (1989-)

Bryant Gumbel - Television Journalist, Sportscaster (1948-)

Fats Domino - Pianist, Singer, Songwriter (1928-)

Terry Bradshaw - Football Player, Athlete, Television Personality (1948-)

Michael DeBakey-Doctor, Educator, Inventor, Surgeon (1908-2008)

Ellen DeGeneres - Talk Show Host, Animal Rights Activist, Comedian (1948-)

Reese Witherspoon - Actress, Producer, Philanthropist (1976-)

Van Cliburn - Pianist (1934-2013)

Interesting Information

- The Louisiana State Capitol in Baton Rouge, at 450 ft., is the tallest state capitol building in the United States. It has 34 floors.

- Louisiana is the only state that does not have counties. The political subdivisions are called parishes.

- Metairie is the home of the longest bridge over water in the world, the Lake Pontchatrain Causeway. The causeway is 24 miles long.

- *Bayou* is a French name for "slow-moving river."

- The Superdome in New Orleans is the world's largest steel-constructed room unobstructed by posts.

*****

For all that is jazz, Bourbon Street in New Orleans is the place to visit. Slaves constructed many of the buildings in the French Quarter, the original walled city of New Orleans. Preservation Hall with the best in traditional jazz for all ages is in the French Quarter. You may want to visit the Amistad Research Center at Tulane University, which has the largest collection of materials on race relations in the United States.

MAINE

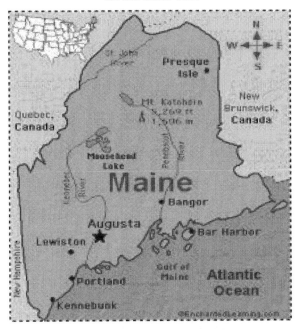

23rd State / March 15, 1820 / Rank in area sq. miles: 39

Nickname: Pine Tree State

Capital: Augusta

Most populous cities: Portland, Lewiston, Bangor

Attractions: Arcadia National Park, Bar Harbor, on Mt. Desert Island; Old Orchard Beach; Old Port historic waterfront, Victoria Mansion, in Portland;

Portland Head Light, in Cape Elizabeth; Maine Maritime Museum, in Bath; L.L. Bean flagship store and outlet shopping, John Brown Russwurm Afro-American Center Library at Bowdoin College, Harriet Beecher Stowe House, in Brunswick

Things to see and places to visit in the most populous cities:

Portland - Portland Museum of Art, Eartha (world's largest revolving globe), Southworth Planetarium at the University of South Maine, Victoria Mansion, Wadsworth-Longfellow House, Scenic Cruise on Casco Bay, Floating Restaurant, Portland Observatory, Portland Head Light, John B. Russwurm House* (second African American in the nation to receive a college degree and co-edited first Black newspaper)

Lewiston - Atrium Art Gallery, University of Southern Maine, Bates College Museum of Art, Basilica of Saints Peter and Paul

111

Bangor - Cole Land Transportation Museum, Paul Bunyan Statue, Maine Discovery Museum

Well-known "Down Easters" and residents:

Henry Wadsworth Longfellow - Poet, Author (1807-1882)

Stephen King - Author (1947-)

Nelson Rockefeller - Governor, U. S. Vice President (1908-1979)

Margaret Chase Smith - U.S. Senator (1897-1995)

Patrick Dempsey - Film Actor, Television Actor (1966-)

David E. Kelley - Television Producer, Screenwriter (c.1956-)

Interesting Information

- A large part of Maine has no roads.
- It is the only state that shares its border with only one state (New Hampshire).
- Maine lies farther east than any other state.

- Maine is the only state in the United States whose name has one syllable, and it is the only state whose official flower, the pinecone, is not a flower.
- Bath is known as the City of Ships.
- Augusta is the most eastern capital in the United States.
- Ninety percent of the country's toothpick supply is produced in Maine.

*****

After you enjoy the delicious seafood and cruise Casco Bay in Portland, you may want to visit the John B. Russwurm House and Harriet Beecher Stowe House in Brunswick. Russwurm was the second African American in the nation to receive a college degree, and he founded and co-edited *Freedom's Journal*, the nation's first black newspaper. Stowe wrote her famous novel on slavery, *Uncle Tom's Cabin* (1852), in Brunswick.

Maine is a scenic seacoast vacationland. From the iconic lighthouses perched along sparkling bays to Portland's cobblestone streets, Maine offers the traveler a unique experience. If you enjoy the seacoast, Maine is a state to visit.

MARYLAND

7th State / April 28, 1788 / Rank in area
sq. miles: 42

Nickname: Old Line State, Free State

Capital: Annapolis

Most populous cities: Baltimore, Columbia, Germantown

Attractions: Ocean City; Ft. McHenry; Pimplico Race Course (Preakness Stakes), Edgar Allen Poe House and Museum, Oriole Park at Camden Yards, National Aquarium, Inner Harbor, The National

Great Blacks in Wax Museum*, Henry Lee Moon Library/NAACP National Civil Rights Archives*, Morgan State University James E. Lewis Museum of Art*, Eubie Blake Cultural Center*, Douglass Place, in Baltimore; Antietam National Battlefield, U.S. Naval Academy, Maryland State House (oldest in continuous legislative use in U.S.), Banneker-Douglass Museum*, in Annapolis; National Cryptologic Museum, Ft. Meade, John Brown's Headquarters* in Samples Manor; Harriet Tubman Birthplace Marker*, 8 miles south of Cambridge on MD 397; Matthew Henson Memorial*, Maryland State House

Things to see and places to visit in the most populous cities:

Baltimore - American Visionary Art Museum, Fort McHenry National Monument and Historic Shrine, Baltimore Museum of Art, Fell's Point, Baltimore and Ohio Railroad Museum, Johns Hopkins University, Oriole Park at Camden Yards, National

116

Aquarium, Harbor Place; Maryland Science Center, The National Great Blacks in Wax Museum*; National Civil Rights Archives*; Morgan State University James E. Lewis Museum of Art*; Eubie Blake Cultural Center*; Douglass Place

Columbia - African Art Museum of Maryland*, Columbia Art Center

Well-known Marylanders and residents:

Reginald F. Lewis - Business Leader, Entrepreneur (1942-1993)

Harriet Tubman - Civil Rights Activist (1820-1913)

Frederick Douglass - Civil Rights Activist (1818-1895)

Matthew Henson - Explorer (1866-1955)

Eubie Blake - Pianist, Songwriter (1887-1983)

Thurgood Marshall - Civil Rights Activist, Lawyer, Supreme Court Justice, Judge (1908-1993)

Kevin Durant - Basketball Player (1988-)

Kweisi Mfume - Civil Rights Activist, U.S. Representative (1948-)

Benjamin Banneker - Astronomer, Scientist (1731-1806)

E. Franklin Frazier - Sociologist (1894-1962)

Nancy Pelosi - Government Official (1940-)

Pete Sampras - Tennis Player (1971-)

Emily Post - Writer (1872-1960)

Sargent Shriver - Legal Professional, Diplomat, Military Activist (1915-2011)

Michael Phelps - Swimmer, Athlete (1985-)

Interesting Information

- Benjamin Banneker designed and built America's first clock in 1753.

- The first dental school in the U.S. opened at the University of Maryland.

- The U.S. Naval Academy is located in Annapolis.

- The National Aquarium is located in Baltimore's Inner Harbor.

- Annapolis is known as the sailing capital of the world.

- Maryland gave up some of its land to form Washington, D.C.

- The first umbrella factory in America was established in Baltimore in 1828.

- The first post office system in the United States was inaugurated in Baltimore in 1774.

- The first telegraph line in the world was established between Washington, D.C., and Baltimore in 1844.

- It is the wealthiest state in the country, as measured by median household incomes.

*****

Baltimore's Inner Harbor offers more to see and do than you could ever imagine. You can take a cruise, visit the National Aquarium, Ft. McHenry National Monument, and much more.

The beautiful Maryland State House is the oldest capitol still in legislative use and the only state house ever to have served as the nation's capital. The Naval Academy at Annapolis is not just for midshipmen; it is open to visitors. It is a tour you may want to take. The University of Maryland has a beautiful campus at College Park.

A visit to The National Great Blacks in Wax Museum in Baltimore is encouraged. It was established in 1983 and features prominent African-American historical figures.

MASSACHUSETTS

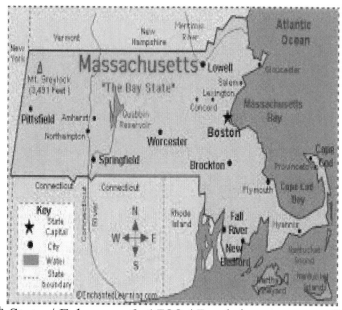

6th State / February 6, 1788 / Rank in area sq. miles: 44

Nickname: Bay State, Old Colony

Capital: Boston

Most populous cities: Boston, Worcester, Springfield, Cambridge

Attractions: Cape Code, Plymouth Rock, *Mayflower II*, in Plymouth; Freedom Trail, Museum of Fine Arts, New England Aquarium, Faneuil Hall,

Boston Public Garden, in Boston; Tanglewood, Berkshire Scenic Railway Museum, Norman Rockwell Museum in the Berkshires region; Peabody Essex Museum, House of the Seven Gables, in Salem; Walden Pond, Louisa May Alcott's Orchard House, in Concord; Naismith Memorial Basketball Hall of Fame, in Springfield; William E. B. DuBois Boyhood Home Site*, in Great Barrington; Boston African American National Historic Site*; African Meeting House*; Crispus Attucks Monument*, Black Heritage Trail*, in Boston; Museum of the National Center of Afro-American Artists*, in Boston; Jan Ernest Matzeliger Monument*, in Lynn

Things to see and places to visit in the most populous cities:

Boston - Freedom Trail, Home of Paul Revere, Old North Church, Old State House Museum, Faneuil Hall Marketplace, Beacon Hill and Charles Street, Fenway Park, *USS Constitution* - Charleston Navy

Yard, Copley Square, Boston Common, New England Aquarium, Chinatown, Cheers, Hancock Tower; Boston African American National Historic Site*, African Meeting House* in Boston's Beacon Hill District, Crispus Attucks Monument*, Black Heritage Trail*, Museum of the National Center of Afro-American Artists*

Worcester - Massachusetts Vietnam Veterans Memorial, FDR Heritage Center, Worcester Art Museum

Springfield - Dr. Seuss National Memorial Sculpture Garden, Basketball Hall of Fame, Springfield College, Pan African Historical Museum U.S.A.*

Cambridge - Harvard, Massachusetts Institute of Technology, Charles River, Harvard Museum of Natural History, Harvard Yard, Harvard Art Museum, MIT Museum

Well-known "Bay Staters" and residents:

Crispus Attucks - Folk Hero (1723-1770)

James Van Der Zee - Photographer (1886-1983)

Donna Summer - Singer, Songwriter (1948-2012)

Lewis Howard Latimer - Inventor, Engineer (1848-1928)

Dorothy West - Author, Editor (1907-1998)

W.E.B. DuBois - Educator, Civil Rights Activist, Journalist (1868-1963)

Robert Lowell - Civil Rights Activist, Anti-War Activist, Poet (1917-1977)

Leonard Bernstein - Pianist, Songwriter, Conductor (1918-1990)

John Hancock - U.S. Representative, U.S. Governor (1737-1793)

Wendell Phillips - Civil Rights Activist (1811-1884)

Leslie Stahl - News Anchor, Editor, Journalist (1941-)

Katherine Lee Bates - Poet, Scholar (1859-1929)

Barbara Walters - News Anchor, Television Producer, Journalist (1929-)

Interesting Information

- Norfolk County is the birthplace of four presidents: John Fitzgerald Kennedy, John Adams, John Quincy Adams, George Herbert Walker Bush.

- The first basketball game was played in Springfield.

- John F. Kennedy was born in Brookline.

- A charter was granted to Harvard College (1644), the oldest college in the U.S.

- The first Thanksgiving Day celebration was in Plymouth in 1621.

- Boston built the first subway system in the United States in 1897.

- There is a house in Rockport built entirely of newspaper.

- The first U.S. Postal ZIP code in Massachusetts is 01001 at Agawam.

- The birth control pill was invented at Clark University in Worcester.
- In 1887, Massachusetts was the first state to require separate toilets for males and females.
- Quincy boasts the first Dunkin Donuts on Hancock Street and the first Howard Johnson's on Newport Avenue.
- Sixteen of the top 25 windiest U.S. cities are located in Massachusetts.

*****

Boston is a city where there is an abundance of historical sites. There is Boston Public Garden, Boston Common, *U.S. Constitution* (*Old Ironsides*), African Meeting House in Boston's Beacon Hill, Crispus Attucks Monument, Freedom Trail, etc. The Freedom Trail is a great way to explore the city; just follow the red brick trail; I did. The John F. Kennedy Presidential Library and Museum in Boston was the first presidential library I visited.

The *Freedom 7*, the space capsule, which took Alan Shepard into space in 1961, is there.

Harvard Square with all its activities is adjacent to Harvard Yard, the historic heart of Harvard University. Each year, over 8 million people visit Harvard Square for a variety of reasons because it is a place of history, books, ideas, and learning. It is a place of bookstores, coffee houses, fine dining, and shopping.

Eight U.S. presidents attended Harvard: John Adams, John Quincy Adams, Rutherford B. Hayes, Theodore Roosevelt, Franklin Delano Roosevelt, John F. Kennedy, George W. Bush, and Barack Obama.

MIT, the private research university, is in Cambridge. It extends over a mile along the northern bank of the Charles River Basin. As of 2015, MIT has produced 85 Nobel Laureates, 52 National Medical of Science recipients, 65 Marshal Scholars,

45 Rhodes Scholars, 38 MacArthur Fellows, and 34 astronauts.

On our way from Cape Cod, we stopped in the town of Plymouth to see the rock inscribed with 1620, the year the Pilgrims landed in the *Mayflower*.

MICHIGAN

26th State / January 26, 1837 / Rank in area sq. miles: 11

Nickname: Great Lakes State, Wolverine State

Capital: Lansing

Most populous cities: Detroit, Grand Rapids, Ann Arbor

Attractions: Henry Ford Museum and Greenfield Village, in Dearborn; Frederik Meijer Gardens and Sculpture Park, in Grand Rapids; Tahquamenon

Falls (of Longfellow's poem *Song of Hiawatha*); De Zwaan Windmill, Tulip Time Festival, in Holland; Soo Locks (between Lakes Superior and Huron), in Sault Ste. Marie; Air Zoo, in Portage; Mackinac Island; Belle Isle, Detroit Institute of Arts, Charles H. Wright Museum of African- American History*, Motown Historical Museum, in Detroit; Sojourner Truth Memorial*, in Battle Creek; Joe Louis Memorials*, National Museum of the Tuskegee Airman*, in Detroit

Things to see and places to visit in the most populous cities:

Detroit - Detroit Institute of Art, Henry Ford Estate, GM Renaissance Center, Motown Museum*, Charles H. Wright Museum of African American History*, Henry Ford Museum and Greenfield Village, Belle Isle, Walter P. Chrysler Museum, Joe Louis Memorials*, Museum of the Tuskegee Airman*

Grand Rapids - Frederik Meijer Gardens and Sculpture Park, Gerald R. Ford Presidential Museum, Grand Rapids Public Museum

Ann Arbor - Dexter Cider Mill, University of Michigan Campus, Michigan Stadium (The Big House), Michigan Football Game, Exhibit Museum of Natural History

Well-known Michiganders and residents:

Della Reese - Singer, Television Actress, Television Host (c.1931-)

Serena Williams - Tennis Player, Athlete (1981-)

Tony Dungy - Football Player, Coach (1955-)

Stevie Wonder - Singer, Pianist, Songwriter (1950-)

Jackie Wilson - Singer (1934-1984)

Diana Ross - Actress, Singer (1944-)

Smokey Robinson - Singer (1940-)

Sugar Ray Robinson - Boxer (1921-1989)

Barry Gordy, Jr. - Director, Producer, Entrepreneur (1929-)

Ralph Bunche - Diplomat (1904-1971)

Floyd Mayweather - Boxer (1977-)

Burt Reynolds - Film Actor, Television Actor (1936-)

Charles Lindberg - Writer, Inventor, Pilot (1902-1974)

Henry Ford - American Industrialist (1863-1947)

Marlo Thomas - Television Actress (1937-)

Madonna - Film Actress, Singer (1958-)

Interesting Information

- Detroit is known as the car capital of the world.

- In 1817 the University of Michigan was the first university established by any of the states.

- Michigan has more shoreline than any other state except Alaska.

- Michigan is the only place in the world with a floating post office. The *J.W. Westcott II* is the only boat in the world that delivers mail to ships while they are still underway. They have been operating for 125 years.

- Standing anywhere in the state, a person is within 85 miles of one of the Great Lakes.
- Michigan was the first state to provide in its Constitution for the establishment of public libraries.
- In 1929, the Michigan State Police established the first police radio system in the world.
- The first auto traffic tunnel built between two nations was the mile-long Detroit-Windsor Tunnel under the Detroit River.

*****

The Henry Ford Museum, Greenfield Village, in Dearborn has displays showing the interaction of agriculture and industry in American life. Several historic structures in the museum relate to African-American history because black families once lived in some of them. The Henry Ford Museum contains inventions of black scientist Elijah McCoy. The bus

Mrs. Rosa Parks rode on February 1, 1955, in Montgomery, AL, and refused to give up her seat is on exhibit there.

The Motown Museum is in Detroit. The famed Motown sound began in 1957 when songwriter Barry Gordy, Jr. quit his job at the Ford Motor Company. Well-known stars and future stars - the Supremes, Michael Jackson, the Four Tops, Smokey Robinson and the Miracles, the Temptations, Lionel Richie, the Commodores, Stevie Wonder, the Spinners, and Gladys Knight and the Pips - recorded at Detroit's Studio A between 1959 and 1972.

Visitors come from across America and throughout the world to stand in Studio A in Motown, where favorite artists and groups recorded their much-loved music. I was in awe when I visited Motown. What an experience! I will always love the Motown Sound.

MINNESOTA

32nd State / May 11, 1858 / Rank in area sq. miles: 12

Nickname: North Star State, Gopher State

Capital: St. Paul

Most populous cities: Minneapolis, St. Paul, Rochester

Attractions: Minneapolis Institute of Arts, Walker Art Center, Minneapolis Sculpture Garden,

Minnehaha Falls (in Longfellow's poem *Song of Hiawatha)*, Guthrie Theater, in Minneapolis; Mall of America, in Bloomington; Ordway Center for the Performing Arts, Science Museum of Minnesota, in St. Paul; Mayo Clinic, in Rochester; North Shore (Lake Superior); Lake Minnetonka; Aerial Lift Bridge, in Duluth

Things to see and places to visit in the most populous cities:

Minneapolis - Minneapolis Institute of Arts, Guthrie Theater, Frederick R. Weisman Art Museum at the University of Minnesota, Minneapolis Sculpture Garden, Walker Art Center, City Hall, Mall of America, Lake Calhoun

St. Paul - Cathedral of St. Paul, Cosmo Park Zoo and Conservatory Science Museum of Minnesota, State Capitol, James J. Hill House, Landmark Center

Rochester - Mayo Clinic, Soldiers Field Veterans Memorial, Plummer House

Well-known Minnesotans and residents:

Prince - Singer, Music Producer, Songwriter (1958-2016)

Toni Stone - Baseball Player, Athlete (1921-1996)

Charles Schultz - Writer, Illustrator (1922-2000)

F. Scott Fitzgerald - Author (1896-1940)

J. Paul Getty - Art Collector, Philanthropist (1892-1976)

William O. Douglas - Government Official, Educator, Lawyer, Supreme Court Justice, Judge (1898-1980)

Warren Burger - Supreme Court Justice (1907-1995)

E. G. Marshall - Actor (c.1914-1998)

Interesting Information

- The Mall of America is the size of 78 football fields.

- Minnesota has 90,000 miles of shoreline, more than California, Florida, and Hawaii combined.

- The following inventions are from Minnesota: Masking and Scotch tape, Wheaties cereal, Bisquick, HMOs, the bundt pan, Aveda beauty products, Green Giant vegetables.

- Minneapolis' famed skyway system connecting 52 blocks (nearly 5 miles) of downtown makes it possible to live, eat, work and shop without going outside.

- The nation's first Better Business Bureau was founded in Minneapolis in 1912.

- The first open heart surgery and the first bone marrow transplant in the United States were performed at the University of Minnesota.

- The stapler was invented in Spring Valley.

- The first automatic pop-up toaster was marketed in June 1926 by McGraw Electric Co. in Minneapolis.

- In 1919, Minneapolis manufactured the nation's first armored cars.
- The first intercollegiate basketball game was played in Minneapolis on February 9, 1895.
- This "Land of 10,000 Lakes" technically has more than 11,000.

*****

When you visit Minneapolis, it is almost a two-for-one of places to visit. You have the Minnesota State Capitol and the Cathedral of Saint Paul in St. Paul. In Minneapolis you have the Skyway System, the University of Minnesota, and Guthrie Theater. The Mall of America is in Bloomington with an inside amusement park and over 500 stores.

A well-known resident of Minneapolis was the late artist Prince, who had a purple rain career. He passed on my birthday.

MISSISSIPPI

20th State/ December 10, 1818 / rank in area sq. miles: 32

Nickname: Magnolia State

Capital: Jackson

Most populous cities: Jackson, Gulfport, Hattiesburg

Attractions: Vicksburg National Military Park; Smith Robertson Museum and Cultural Center; Mardi Gras parades of Gulfport, Gulf Island

National Seashore; Delta Blues Museum, in Clarksdale; Natchez Trace Parkway, Alcorn State University campus - Oakland Chapel*, Mississippi State Capitol, University of Mississippi Blues Archive in Oxford

Things to see and places to visit in the most populous cities:

Jackson - Mississippi Museum of Natural Science, Mississippi Museum of Art, Mississippi Sports Hall of Fame, Medgar Evers Home*, Jackson State University*, Cathedral of St. Peter the Apostle, City Hall, Old Capitol Museum, War Memorial Building, Russell C. Davis Planetarium, State Capitol

Gulfport - Busted Wrench Garage Museum, City Hall

Hattiesburg - Mississippi Armed Forces Museum, African American Military History Museum*

Well-known Mississippians and residents:

Ida B. Wells - Civil Rights Activist, Journalist (1862-1931)

Leontyne Price - Singer (1927-)

Fannie Lou Hamer - Civil Rights Activist, Philanthropist (1917-1977)

Richard Wright - Poet, Author, Journalist (1908-1960)

James Earl Jones - Film Actor, Theater Actor (1931-)

B.B. King - Singer, Guitarist, Songwriter (1925-2015)

Medgar Evers - Civil Rights Activist (1925-1963)

David Ruffin - Singer (1941-1991)

Oprah Winfrey - Film Actress, Talk Show Host, Television Producer, Philanthropist (1954-)

William Grant Sill - Conductor, Songwriter (1895-1978)

Walter Payton - Football Player, Athlete (1954-1999)

James Meredith - Civil Rights Activist (1933-)

Bo Diddley - Singer, Guitarist, Songwriter (1928-2008)

Sam Cooke - Songwriter, Singer (1931-1964)

Cool Papa Bell - Baseball Player (1903-1991)

Robert L. Johnson - American Entrepreneur (1946-)

Tavis Smiley - Philanthropist, Radio Talk Show Host, Journalist (1964-)

Tennessee Williams - Playwright (1911-1983)

Tammy Wynette - Singer, Guitarist, Songwriter (1942-1998)

Conway Twitty - Singer, Songwriter (1933-1993)

Faith Hill - Singer (1967-)

William Faulkner - Author (1897-1962)

Interesting Information

- Mississippi was the first state in the nation to have a planned system of junior colleges.

- The Vicksburg National Cemetery is the second largest national cemetery in the country. The Arlington National Cemetery is the largest.
- Pine Sol was invented in 1929 by Jackson native Harry Cole, Jr.
- Root Beer was invented in Biloxi in 1898 by Edward Adolf Barq, Sr.
- The largest Bible-binding plant in the nation is Norris Bookbinding Company in Greenwood.
- Mississippi is the birthplace of the Order of Eastern Star.

*****

It occurred to me that I have spent very little time in Mississippi. Perhaps it had to do with my pre-1965 experience traveling through the state with my uncle. My more recent visit was to the Gulf Coast, which was most enjoyable. In addition to stopping by the capitol in Jackson, if you are a history buff, you may want to visit the Vicksburg

National Military Park and Cemetery. The cemetery is the nation's largest burial site of Civil War Union soldiers and sailors. There is the B. B. King Museum and Delta Interpretive Center in Indianola. Then, there is Ole Miss at Oxford, the school which James M. Meredith attended. He was a civil rights activist who became nationally renowned in 1962, when he became the first African-American student at the University of Mississippi.

MISSOURI

24th State / August 10, 1821 / Rank in area sq. miles: 21

Nickname: Show Me State

Capital: Jefferson City

Most populous cities: Kansas City, St. Louis, Springfield, Independence

Attractions: Silver Dollar City, in Branson; Mark Twain Boyhood Home and Museum, in Hannibal; Pony Express National Museum, in St. Joseph; Harry S. Truman Library and Museum, in Independence; Gateway Arch (part of Jefferson

National Expansion Memorial), National Blues Museum, Ulysses S. Grant National Historic Site, St. Louis Zoo, The Black Archives of Mid-America*, Kansas City; Worlds of Fun amusement park, in Kansas City; Lake of the Ozarks; Ozark National Scenic River Ways; State Capitol, in Jefferson City; George Washington Carver National Monument*, Diamond; Scott Joplin House*, in St. Louis

Things to see and places to visit in the most populous cities:

Kansas City - National World War I Museum at Liberty Memorial, Kemper Museum, Museum of Contemporary Art, Hall Visitor Center, Airline History Museum, The Black Archives of Mid-America*

St. Louis - Gateway Arch, Jefferson National Expansion Memorial Park, Old Courthouse, National Blues Museum, Missouri Botanical

Garden, City Museum, Scott Joplin House*, Lumiere Sculpture Park, St. Louis Zoo, St. Louis Science Center, The Missouri History Museum, Anheuser Busch Brewery Tour, Cathedral Basilica of St. Louis, Busch Stadium, Ulysses S. Grant National Historical Site

Springfield - Nathanael Greene/Close Memorial Park, Springfield Botanical Gardens, Missouri Sports Hall of Fame

Independence - UN Peace Plaza, Truman Museum and Library, Harry S. Truman National Historic Site

Well-known Missourians and residents:

George Washington Carver - Inventor, Botanist, Scientist (c.1864-1943)

Maya Angelou - Poet, Author, Civil Rights Activist (1928-2014)

Langston Hughes - Poet, Playwright (1902-1967)

Roy Wilkins - Civil Rights Activist, Editor, Journalist (1901-1981)

Dick Gregory - Civil Rights Activist, Comedian (1932-)

Redd Fox - Film Actor, Television Actor, Comedian (1922-1991)

Josephine Baker - Singer, Dancer, Civil Rights Activist (1906-1975)

Faye Wattleton - Business Leader, Women's Rights Activist, Nurse, Philanthropist (1943-)

JC Penney - Philanthropist (1875-1971)

Jane Wyman - Actress (1917-2007)

Ed Asner - Animal Rights Activist, Television Actor (1929-)

Omar Bradley - General (1893-1981)

Dale Carnegie - Author (1888-1955)

Walter Cronkite - News Anchor, Journalist (1916-2009)

T.S. Eliot - Writer (1888-1965)

Edwin Hubble - Astronomer, Scientist (1889-1953)

Doris Roberts - Film Actress, Television Actress (1925-2016)

Harry Truman - U.S. President (1884-1972)

Bill Bradley - Basketball Player, U.S. Representative, U.S. Senator (1943-)

Interesting Information

- Bordered by eight states, Missouri ties with Tennessee as the most neighborly state in the Union.

- Kansas City has more miles of boulevards than Paris and more fountains than any city except Rome.

- Kansas City has more miles of freeway per capita than any metro area with more than 1 million residents.

- In 1865 Missouri became the first slave state to free its slaves.

*****

In the Trolley Song "Meet Me in St. Louis", Judy Garland tells the listener to meet her there. Well, you may want to tell a friend to do the same because there is a lot to do and see in St. Louis. There is Busch Stadium, Ulysses S. Grant National Historic Site, Jefferson National Expansion Memorial Park, and the iconic Gateway Arch. The Arch rises to a height of 630-feet and gives quite a view of the city.

Union Station is in St. Louis. It is a National Historic Landmark and was once the world's largest and busiest train station. The Old Court House, the historical landmark where Dred and Harriet Scott sued for freedom from slavery and where Virginia Minor fought for women's right to vote, is there. The George Washington Carver National Monument is in Diamond.

Like St. Louis, there is a lot to see and do in Kansas City. I enjoyed visiting the Jazz Museum and the Negro League's Baseball Hall of Fame. Hallmark Cards' - when you care to send the very best - headquarters are in Kansas City. There are many great barbecue restaurants in KC, but two I enjoyed were Gates Bar-B-Q and Arthur Bryant's.

The Truman Presidential Library and Museum is a short distance away in Independence. With its very popular message, Truman's "The Buck Stops Here!" desk sign is on display.

MONTANA

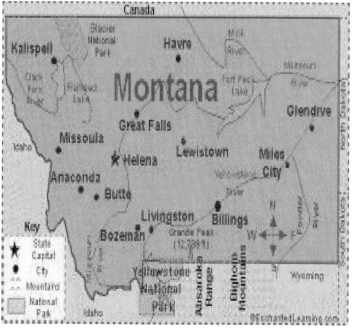

41ˢᵗ State / November 8, 1889 / Rank in

area sq. miles: 4

Nickname: Treasure State

Capital: Helena

Most populous cities: Billings, Missoula, Great

Falls

Attractions: Glacier and Yellowstone National

Parks, Museum of the Rockies, in Bozeman;

Museum of the Plains Indian, Blackfeet Reservation,

in Browning; Custer National Cemetery at Little Bighorn Battlefield National Monument; Lewis and Clark Caverns State Park, Whitehall; Lewis and Clark National Historic Trail Interpretative Center, Great Falls

Things to see and places to visit in the most populous cities:

Billings - Moss Mansion, Little Bighorn Battlefield National Monument

Missoula - University of Montana, Missoula Art Museum

Great Falls - Lewis and Clark Interpretative Center

Well-known Montanans and residents:

Chet Huntley - Television Newscaster (1911-1974)

Myrna Loy - Film Actress, Television Actress, Stage Actress (1905-1993)

Mike Mansfield - U.S. Senator, Diplomat (1903-2001)

Brent Musburger - Sportscaster (1939-)

Steve Reeves - Film Actor, Athlete (1926-2000)

David Lynch - Director, Screenwriter (1946-)

Evel Knievel - Actor, Athlete (1938-2007)

Gary Cooper - Film Actor (1901-1961)

Patrick Duffy - Television Actor (1949-)

Phil Jackson - Coach (1945-)

Interesting Information

- Montana is larger than Japan, United Kingdom and Italy. If Montana were to secede from the Union, it would be the 62nd largest country in the world.

- Forty-six of Montana's 56 counties are considered "frontier counties" with an average of 6 or fewer people per square mile.

- Yellowstone National Park in southern Montana and northern Wyoming was the first national park in the nation.

- Montana is home to seven Indian reservations.

- The Going to the Sun Run in Glacier National Park is considered one of the most scenic drives in America.
- Glacier National Park has 250 lakes within its boundaries.
- Mile City is known as the Cowboy Capital.
- Montana is the only state bordering three Canadian provinces: Saskatchewan, Alberta, and British Columbia.
- A Gideon bible was first placed inside a hotel in Montana.

*****

Montana is not called "Big Sky Country" without a reason. It is the 4th largest state in square mileage, but it is one of the ten smallest in population. The lure of Yellowstone National Park is a large source of Boseman, Montana's, tourism. Established in 1872, Yellowstone is America's first national park and is located in Wyoming, Montana, and Idaho. In addition to Yellowstone, you may want to add the Grand Teton National Park and Glacier National Park to your list when you visit Montana.

NEBRASKA

37th State / March 1, 1867 / Rank in area sq. miles: 16

Nickname: Cornhusker State

Capital: Lincoln

Most populous cities: Omaha, Lincoln, Bellevue

Attractions: University of Nebraska State Museum at Morrill Hall, Nebraska Capitol, in Lincoln; Stuhr Museum of the Prairie Pioneer, in Grand Island; Boys Town; Doorly Zoo and Aquarium, Joslyn Art Museum, The Durham Museum, Malcolm X House

Site,* Black Americana Museum,* Great Plains Black Museum,* in Omaha; Strategic Air and Space Museum, in Ashland; Buffalo Bill Ranch State Historical Park, in North Platte; Oregon Trail landmarks, included at Scotts Bluff National Monument and Chimney Rock Historic Site; Museum of Nebraska Art, in Kearney

Things to see and places to visit in the most populous cities:

Omaha - Henry Doorly Zoo and Aquarium, Old Market District, First National's Spirit of Nebraska's Wilderness and Pioneer Courage Park, Saint Cecilia Cathedral, Boys Town, Strategic Air and Space Museum, Malcolm X House Site*, Black Americana Museum*, Great Plains Black Museum*, in Omaha

Lincoln - The World of Quilts, Morrill Hall, Drive Down "O" Street, State Capitol, Visit the East Campus of the University of Nebraska, Memorial

Stadium, Sunken Gardens, Nebraska History Museum, UNL

Well-known Nebraskans and residents:

Malcolm X (born Malcolm Little) - Civil Rights Activist, Minister (1925-1965)

Arthur Godfrey - Film Actor, Television Actor, Comedian, Television Personality (1969-)

Darryl F. Zanuck - Producer (1902-1979)

Ted Sorensen - Writer, Lawyer (1928-2010)

Gerald Ford - Lawyer, U.S. Representative, U.S. Vice President, U.S. President (1913-2006)

Henry Fonda - Film Actor, Theater Actor, Television Actor (1905-1982)

Montgomery Clift - Film Actor (1920-1966)

Interesting Information

- Nebraska is the birthplace of the Reuben sandwich.
- Spam (canned meat) is produced in Fremont.

- The 911 system of emergency communications, now used nationwide, was developed and first used in Lincoln

- In 1950, Omaha became the home of the College World Series.

- In 1957, Edwin E. Perkins of Hastings invented the powdered soft drink Kool-Aid.

- Nebraska is the only state in the Union with a unicameral (one house) legislature.

- The largest porch swing in the world is located in Hebron and it can sit 25 adults.

*****

The Nebraska State Capitol in downtown Lincoln is the top attraction at 400 feet tall; it is known as the "Tower on the Plains." It can be seen as far away as 30 miles. It is the second tallest U.S. state house in the country. Memorial Stadium in Lincoln, home of the University of Nebraska Huskers, is a favorite during football season. Lincoln is known as Silicon Prairie. Boys Town is in

Omaha and the College World Series in baseball is played there in June of each year.

NEVADA

36th State / October 31, 1864 / Rank in area sq. miles: 7

Nickname: Sagebrush State, Battle Born State, Silver State

Capital: Carson City

Most populous cities: Las Vegas, Henderson, North Las Vegas, Reno

Attractions: Hoover Dam, Lake Mead National Recreation Area, near Boulder City; Great Basin

National Park; Valley of Fire State Park; Las Vegas Strip, Fremont Street, National Atomic Testing Museum, Pinball Hall of Fame, Las Vegas Motor Speedway, in Las Vegas; National Automobile Museum, in Reno

Things to see in the most populous cities:

Las Vegas - Las Vegas Strip, Fremont Street Experience, Las Vegas Natural History Museum, University of Nevada, Thomas and Mack Center at UNLV, Walker African American Museum*, Lake Mead and Hoover Dam, Bellagio Fountains, MGM Grand (3rd largest hotel in the world)

Henderson - Ethel M. Chocolate Factory and Botanical Cactus Gardens, Clark County Heritage Museum

Reno - National Automobile Museum, Wilbur D. May Museum, Arboretum and Botanical Gardens, Sierra Safari Zoo, University of Nevada, Lake Tahoe, Powning Veterans Memorial Park, 1920's -

1940's Cars at National Automobile Museum, N. Virginia Street

Well-known Nevadans and residents:

Rutina Wesley - Film Actress, Theater Actress, Television Actress (1970-)

Pat Nixon - U.S. First Lady, Children's Activist (1912-1993)

Harry Reid - Governmental Official, Lawyer, U.S. Representative, U.S. Senator (1939-)

Andre Agassi - Tennis Player (1970-)

Kyle Busch - Race Car Driver (1985-)

Key Pittman - U.S. Senator (1878-1920)

Interesting Information

- Gambling was legalized in the state in 1931.
- Nevada has more mountain ranges than any other state.
- Las Vegas has more hotel rooms than any other place on earth.
- The majority of the largest hotels in the world are in Las Vegas.

- Virginia City is the home of the Nevada Gambling Museum.
- Nevada is the largest gold-producing state in the nation. It is second in the world behind South Africa.
- Nevada is the driest state in the nation.
- The MGM Grand in Las Vegas is the largest hotel on the Strip with 5,690 rooms.

*****

Strolling down the Las Vegas Strip is an exhilarating experience. The roller coasters, the rides, hotel shopping malls, restaurants, the Luxor, MGM Grand, Eiffel Tower, the Bellagio's Dancing Fountains, Caesars Palace, the Mandalay Bay's Wave Pool, and the Venetian are a few of the many attractions Las Vegas has to offer. The Las Vegas Strip may be the most exciting place on earth with non-stop fun. Does what happen in Vegas really stay in Vegas? Hoover Dam, a major construction achievement, is about thirty miles from Las Vegas.

166

You may want to visit Reno when you are in the state which claims to be "The Biggest Little City in the World." If you are in Reno, go see the beautiful Lake Tahoe, which has a surface elevation of 6,229 feet and a shoreline of 72 miles in length. It is 22 miles long and 12 miles wide.

NEW HAMPSHIRE

9th State / June 21, 1788 / Rank in area
sq. miles: 46

Nickname: Granite State

Capital: Concord

Most populous cities: Manchester, Nashua, Concord

Attractions: Mt. Washington Cog Railway, Mt. Washington (highest peak in the Northeast), Flume

168

Gorge, Cannon Mountain Aerial Tramway, in the White Mountains regions; Strawberry Banke Museum, in Portsmouth; Canterbury Shaker Village; Saint-Gaudens National Historic Site, in Cornish; Santa's Village, in Jefferson

Things to see and places to visit in the most populous cities:

Manchester - City Hall, Currier Gallery of Art, Currier Museum of Art

Nashua - Fall foliage scenes, White Mountains

Concord - New Hampshire State House, Christa McAuliffe Planetarium, Museum of New Hampshire History

Well-known New Hampshirites and residents:
Allan Shepard - Astronaut (1923-1998)
Horace Greeley - Editor, Journalist (1811-1872)
Daniel Webster - Government Official, Lawyer, U.S. Representative (1782-1852)

Seth Meyers - Actor, Talk Show Host, Comedian, Screenwriter (1973-)

Mandy Moore - Film Actress, Singer (1984-)

Interesting Information

- Levi Hutchins of Concord invented the first alarm clock.

- Of the thirteen original colonies, New Hampshire was the first to declare its independence from Mother England - a full six months before the Declaration of Independence was signed.

- The first potato planted in the United States was at Londonderry Common Field in 1719.

- In 1833, the first free public library in the United States was established in Peterborough.

- New Hampshire adopted the first legal lottery in the twentieth century in the United States in 1963.

- The New Hampshire State House is the oldest state capitol in which the legislature still meets in its original chambers.

- This state's license plates, bearing the slogan "Live Free or Die," are made by prison inmates.

*****

New Hampshire is called "the White Mountains State" because this mountain range runs across the northern portion of the state. All I can say about New Hampshire is I have been in the state, and some of the attractions are Mt. Washington Auto Road, Conway Scenic Railroad, Castle in the Clouds, and the Lakes Region. Horace Greeley, the journalist, was born in New Hampshire and is attributed with the famous quote: "Go West young man, go West."

NEW JERSEY

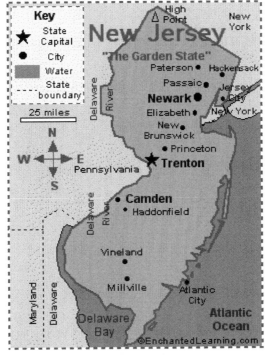

3rd State / December 18, 1787 / Rank in area sq. miles: 47

Nickname: Garden State

Capital: Trenton

Most populous cities: Newark, Jersey City, Patterson

Attractions: Boardwalks on the Jersey Shore at Atlantic City; Seaside Heights; Ocean City; Wildwood; Grover Cleveland Birthplace, Caldwell;

Cape May Historic District; Thomas Edison National Historic Park, in West Orange; Six Flags Great Avenue, in Jackson; Liberty University, Princeton Battlefield State Park, in Princeton; Morristown National Historic Park; Adventure Aquarium; Battleship *New Jersey*, Walt Whitman House, in Camden; Afro-American Historical Museum*, in Jersey City; Paul Robeson Center of Rutgers University at Newark*; African Art Museum of the Society of African Mission Fathers*, in Tenafly

Things to see and places to visit in the most populous cities:

Newark - Liberty State Park, Cathedral Basilica of the Sacred Heart, Prudential Center, Paul Roberson Center of Rutgers University at Newark*

Jersey City - J. Owen Grundy Park, Holland Tunnel, Liberty State Park, Hudson River

Waterfront Walkway, Liberty Science Center, Afro-American Historical Museum*

Well-known New Jerseyans and residents:

Whitney Houston - Film Actress, Singer (1963-2012)

Paul Robeson - Civil Rights Activist, Actor, Football Player (1898-1976)

Malcolm Jamal Warner - Television Actor (1970-)

Alice Paul - Women's Rights Activist (1885-1977)

Rubin "Hurricane" Carter - Boxer (1937-2014)

Queen Latifah - Film Actress, Singer, Rapper, Music Producer, Television Actress (1970-)

Keshia Knight Pulliam - Television Actress (1979-)

Taye Diggs - Actor (1972-)

Shaquille O'Neal - Film Actor, Basketball Player, Rapper (1972-)

Dionne Warwick - Singer (1940-)

Count Basie - Pianist, Songwriter (1904-1984)

Flip Wilson - Actor, Comedian (1933-1998)

Bill Bradley - U.S. Senator, Basketball Player (1943-)

Thomas Paine - Political Activist, Philosopher (1737-1809)

Dave Thomas - Chef, Businessman, Philanthropist (1932-2002)

Walt Whitman - Poet, Journalist (1818-1892)

Woodrow Wilson - U. S. President, Governor (1856-1924)

Thomas Edison - Inventor, Businessman (1847-1931)

Albert Einstein - Physicist, Scientist (1879-1955)

Jack Nicholson - Film Actor, Producer, Writer (1937-)

Steve Forbes - Business Leader, Editor (1947-)

Michael Douglas - Film Actor, Activist, Filmmaker (1944-)

Frank Sinatra - Film Actor, Singer (1915-1998)

Connie Francis - Film Actress, Singer, Television Actress, Television Personality (1938-)

Martha Stewart - Businesswoman, Writer, Television Personality (1941-)

Meryl Streep - Film Actress (1949-)

Interesting Information

- New Jersey has the highest population density in the U.S, an average of 1,030 people per sq. mile, which is 13 times the national average.

- New Jersey is the only state where all its counties are classified as metropolitan areas.

- New Jersey has the most dense system of highways and railroads in the U.S.

- Atlantic City has the longest boardwalk in the world.

- New Jersey has the tallest water tower in the world.

- The first baseball game was played in Hoboken.

- The first Indian reservation was in New Jersey.
- The first drive-in movie theater was opened in Camden.
- New Jersey is one of five smallest states.

*****

The Drifters sing "Under the Boardwalk." If that is where you want to be, then Atlantic City is the place. Also, New Jersey has Ocean City and Cape May. For me, I like visiting beautiful college campuses, and Princeton University is in that category. In Jersey City is the beautiful Liberty State Park. Hoboken is the birthplace of Frank Sinatra, who believed in doing things his way.

Another notable New Jersey resident is Paul Leroy Robeson, who was born in Princeton. Paul Robeson was a famous African-American athlete, singer, actor, scholar, football player, civil rights activist, and lawyer. He used his deep baritone voice to promote Black spirituals, to share the cultures of other countries, and to support the labor and social movements of his time. He sang for peace and justice in 25 languages throughout the U.S., Europe, the Soviet Union, and Africa. In May 1958, on the third anniversary of Brown vs the Board of Education when the prayer *Pilgrimage for Freedom* was convening during the 1957 civil rights assembly at the Lincoln Memorial, I met Robeson and got his autograph.

NEW MEXICO

47th State / January 6, 1912 / Rank in
area sq. miles: 5

Nickname: Land of Enchantment

Capital: Santa Fe

Most populous cities: Albuquerque, Las Cruces,
Santa Fe

Attractions: Carlsbad Caverns National Park (with
Lechuguilla Cave, among world's longest caves);
Sandia Peak Tramway, in Albuquerque; New

179

Mexico History Museum, Museum of International Folk Art, in Santa Fe (oldest U.S. capital); White Sands National Monument (world's largest gypsum dune field); Chaco Culture National Historical Park; Acoma Pueblo, or Sky City, built atop a 367 feet mesa; Taos Art Colony; International UFO Museum and Research Center, in Roswell

Things to see and places to visit in the most populous cities:

Albuquerque - Albuquerque International Balloon Fiesta, Old Town, Indian Pueblo Cultural Center, New Mexico Museum of Natural History and Science, Church of San Flipe de Neri, University of New Mexico

Las Cruces - Farm and Ranch Heritage Museum

Santa Fe - Georgia O'Keeffe Museum, Loretta Chapel, Museum of Indian Arts and Culture, Laboratory of Anthropology, Museum of

International Folk Art, Plaza, New Mexico Capitol, Palace of the Governors

Well-known New Mexicans and residents:

Neil Patrick Harris - Actor (1973-)

John Denver - Environmental Activist, Singer, Guitarist, Songwriter (1943-1997)

Demi Moore - Film Actress, Producer, Director (1962-)

Conrad Hilton – American Hotelier (1887-1979)

Bruce Cabot - Film Actor (1904-1972)

Georgia O'Keeffe - Artist (1887-1986)

Bill Richardson - Governor, U.S. Ambassador (1947-)

Nancy Lopez - Professional Golfer (1957-)

Interesting Information

- Santa Fe, the oldest capital city in the United States, was founded in 1610.

- Santa Fe is the highest capital city in the United States at 7,000 feet above sea level.

- The Rio Grande is the longest river and runs the entire length of New Mexico.

- New Mexico has far more sheep and cattle than people. There are only about 12 people per square miles.

- A third of the people speak Spanish.

- The Palace of the Governors in Santa Fe is the oldest government in the United States.

- The Navajo, the nation's largest Native American group, have a reservation that covers 14 million acres.

- El Camino, built in 1581 in New Mexico, is the oldest road in the United States.

*****

I was impressed with the images of Albuquerque at night; they are magnificent. If you are daring, you may want to ride in a balloon; visit Old Town; ride the Sandia Peak Tramway; or visit the Pueblo Cultural Center, White Sands National Monument, Chaco Cultural National Historical Site, and

Carlsbad Caverns National Park. My visit to Santa
Fe, the oldest capital city in the United States, was
intriguing.

NEW YORK

11th State / July 26, 1788 / Rank in
area sq. miles: 27

Nickname: Empire State

Capital: Albany

Most populous cities: New York, Buffalo,
Rochester

Attractions: New York City; Adirondack and
Catskill Mountains; Watkins Glen State Park;
Niagara Falls; Old Dutch Church of Sleepy Hollow,
in Sleepy Hollow; Washington Irving's Sunnyside,

184

in Tarrytown; Corning Museum of Glass; Fenimore Art Museum; National Baseball Hall of Fame and Museum in Cooperstown; Ft. Ticonderoga; New York State Capitol, in Albany; Home of Franklin D. Roosevelt National Historic Site, in Hyde Park; Long Island beaches; Sagamore Hill (Theodore Roosevelt's "Summer White House"), Oyster Bay, John Roosevelt "Jackie" Robinson House*, Edward Kennedy "Duke" Ellington House*, Langston Hughes House*, James Weldon Johnson House*, Paul Robeson House*, Louis Armstrong House*, Ralph Bunche House*, New York Amsterdam News Building*, Schomburg Center for Research*, in New York City; William Seward House, Harriet Tubman Museum*, in Auburn; Kush Museum of African-American Art and Antiquities*, in Buffalo; Louis Armstrong House and Archives*, in Corona; African American Museum of Nassau County*, in Hempstead; Alpha Phi Alpha Fraternity Founding Home*, in Ithaca; Abyssinian Baptist Church*, Center for African Art* Studio Museum of Harlem*,

Black Fashion Museum*, in New York; Susan B. Anthony House National Historic Landmark, Frederick Douglass Gravesite*, in Rochester

Things to see and places to visit in the most populous cities:

New York City - Statue of Liberty and Battery Park, Empire State Building, Central Park, Broadway and Shubert Alley, Metropolitan Museum of Art, Rockerfeller Center, Fifth Avenue, Brooklyn Bridge, Times Square, Chrysler Building, New York Public Library, Solomon R. Guggenheim Museum, Wall Street, St. Patrick's Cathedral, Bronx Zoo, Lincoln Center, 911 Memorial, American Museum of Natural History, Apollo Theater*, Grand Central Terminal, Radio City Music Hall, Staten Island Ferry, The High Line, John Roosevelt "Jackie" Robinson House*, Edward Kennedy "Duke" Ellington House*, Langston Hughes House*, James Weldon Johnson House*, Paul Robeson Home*, Louis Armstrong House*, Ralph Bunche House*,

New York Amsterdam News Building*, Schomburg Center for Research in Black Culture*; Abyssinian Baptist Church*, Apollo Theater*, Center for African Art*, Studio Museum of Harlem*, Black Fashion Museum*

Buffalo - Buffalo and Erie County Botanical Gardens, Buffalo and Erie County Naval and Military Park, Theodore Roosevelt National Historic Site, St. Joseph's Cathedral, Canalside, Buffalo City Hall

Rochester - George Eastman House, National Susan B. Anthony Museum and House, Strasenburg Planetarium, Rochester Museum and Science Center

Well-known New Yorkers and residents:

Sojourner Truth - Women's Rights Activist, Civil Rights Activist (c.1797-1883)

Harry Belafonte - Civil Rights Activist, Actor (1927-)

Mike Tyson - Boxer (1966-)

Kim Fields - Television Actress (1969-)

J-Z - Rapper, Music Producer (1969-)

Whoopi Goldberg - Film Actress, Talk Show Host, Television Actress, Comedian (1955-)

Al Sharpton - Civil Rights Activist, Pastor (1954-)

Michael Jordan - Basketball Player (1963-)

Clive Davis - Business Leader, Music Producer (1932-)

Vanessa Williams - Actress, Singer (1963-)

Denzel Washington - Film Actor (1954-)

Eddie Murphy - Film Actor, Television Actor, Comedian, Director (1961-)

Sammie Davis, Jr. - Film Actor, Singer, Television Actor, Comedian, Dancer (1925-1990)

James Baldwin - Writer (1924-1987)

Luther Vandross - Singer, Songwriter, Record Producer (1951-2005)

Colin Powell - Diplomat, Military Leader (1937-)

Jane Fonda - Actress (1937-)

Vince Lombardi - Coach (1913-1970)

Jon Stewart - Writer, Talk Show Host, Comedian (1962-)

Charlie Sheen - Film Actor, Television Actor (1965-)

Bill Maher - Animal Rights Activist, Talk Show Host, Comedian (1956-)

Pat Riley - Basketball Player, Football Player, Coach (1945-)

Jackie Kennedy Onassis - U.S. First Lady, Publisher (1929-1994)

Jonas Salk - Doctor, Scientist (1914-1995)

Tony Bennett - Singer (1926-)

Barbara Streisand - Actress, Singer (1942-)

Mark Zuckerberg - Computer Programmer, Philanthropist (1984-)

Lauren Bacall - Film Actress, Theater Actress, Television Actress, Pin-Up (1924-2014)

Robert De Niro - Film Actor, Theater Actor, Director (1943-)

Jimmy Kimmel - Game Show Host, Talk show Host, Comedian (1967-)

Sonia Sotomayor - Lawyer, Supreme Court Justice (1954-)

Franklin D. Roosevelt - U.S. President (1882-1945)

Matt Lauer - Talk Show Host, News Anchor (1957-)

Susan B. Anthony - Women's Rights Activist (1820-1906)

Ruth Bader Ginsburg - Supreme Court Justice (1933-)

Carroll O'Connor - Television Actor, Producer, Director (1924-2001)

Eugene O'Neill - Playwright (1888-1953)

Eleanor Roosevelt - U.S. First Lady (longest serving First Lady of the United States), Diplomat, Activist (1884-1962)

Bernie Sanders - Mayor, U.S. Representative, U.S. Senator (1941-)

Nelson Rockefeller - Businessman, Philanthropist, Governor (1908-1979)

Tom Cruise - Actor, Filmmaker (1962-)

Ray Romano - Actor, Screenwriter, Comedian (1957-)

Humphrey Bogart - Screen Actor (1899-1957)

Donald J. Trump – U.S. President, Business Leader, Television Personality (1946-)

Interesting Information

- Fashion Institute of Technology in Manhattan is the only school in the world offering a Bachelor of Science degree with a major in Cosmetics and Fragrance Marketing.
- New York has 772 miles of subway track.
- New York is the home of the United Nations.
- The 641 mile transportation network known as the Governor Thomas E. Dewey Thruway is the longest toll road in the United States.
- The Big Apple is a term coined by musicians meaning "to play the big time."
- New York was the first state to require license plates on cars.

- The first capital of the United States was New York City.

*****

There was a time when one of my favorite places to walk was 42nd and Broadway. There is so much to see and so much to do in New York City. I have been to some of the world's most famous cities, and there is no place like New York City. From time to time, I meet people who have not been to New York, and my recommendation is see New York. As the saying goes, "If you can make it in New York, you can make it anywhere."

NORTH CAROLINA

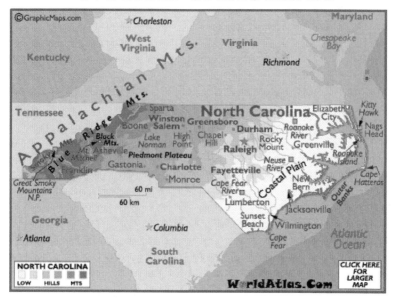

12th State / November 21, 1789 / Rank in area sq.

miles: 28

Nickname: The Tar Heel State, Old North State

Capital: Raleigh

Most populous cities: Charlotte, Raleigh, Greensboro

Attractions: Cape Hatteras and Cape Lookout National Seashores; Great Smoky Mountains National Park; Guilford Courthouse National Military Park; Moore's Creek National Battlefield

(1776 victory ended British rule in colony); Bennett Place (site of the largest troop surrender of the Civil War), in Durham; Ft. Raleigh National Historic Site, North Carolina Aquarium, on Roanoke Island; Wright Brothers National Memorial, in Kill Devil Hills; *USS North Carolina*, in Wilmington; North Carolina Zoo, in Asheboro; North Carolina Museum of Art, North Carolina Museum of Natural Sciences, in Raleigh; Carl Sandburg Home, in Flat Rock; Biltmore House and Gardens, North Carolina Arboretum, in Asheville; Discovery Place, in Charlotte; Charlotte Hawkins Brown Memorial*, in Sedalia; Harvey B. Gantt Center for African-American Arts Culture*, in Charlotte

Things to see and places to visit in the most populous cities:

Charlotte - Carowinds, Levine Museum of the New South, Mint Museum Uptown, NASCAR Hall of Fame, Charlotte Motor Speedway, Billy Graham

Library, Carolinas Aviation Museum, North Carolina Music Factory, Harvey B. Gantt Center for African-American Arts Culture*

Raleigh - The Executive Mansion, North Carolina State University, North Carolina Museum of Natural Sciences, North Carolina Museum of History, North Carolina State Capitol

Greensboro - Greensboro Historical Museum, International Civil Rights Museum*, Greensboro Science Center, North Carolina Agricultural and Technical State University*

Well-known North Carolinians and residents:

Charlotte Hawkins Brown - Educator (1883-1961)

Charles Sifford - Golfer (1922-2015)

Sugar Ray Leonard - Boxer (1956-)

Roberta Flack - Singer, Songwriter (1937-)

Max Roach - Educator, Civil Rights Activist, Drummer, Songwriter (1924-2007)

Floyd Patterson - Boxer (1935-2006)

Clyde McPhatter - Singer (1932-1972)

Jackie "Moms" Mabley - Comedian (1894-1975)

Floyd B. McKissick - Legal Professional, Civil Rights Activist (1922-1991)

Levin Coffin - Activist (1798-1878)

Howard Cosell - Talk Show Host, News Anchor (1918-1995)

Ava Gardner - Film Actress, Pin-up (1922-1990)

Charles Kuralt - Radio Personality, News Anchor, Journalist (1934-1997)

Edward R. Murrow - Radio Personality, News Anchor, Journalist (1908-1965)

Charlie Rose - Talk Show Host, Television Producer, Journalist (1942-)

Billy Graham - Evangelist (1918-)

Andy Griffith - Actor, Talk Show Host, (1926-2012)

Julianne Moore - Actress (c.1960-)

Interesting Information

- The University of North Carolina at Chapel Hill is the oldest state university in the United States.

- High Point is known as the Furniture Capital of the World.

- Krispy Crème, the doughnut company, was founded in Winston-Salem.

- Biltmore Estate in Asheville is America's largest home, having 250 rooms (including 35 bedrooms and 43 bathrooms).

- Babe Ruth hit his first home run in Fayetteville on March 7, 1914.

- The first state-owned art museum in the country is located in Raleigh.

- Pepsi was invented and first served in New Bern in 1898.

- Hiram Revels, born in Fayetteville in 1822, was the first African-American member of Congress in the United States.

- Mt. Mitchell (6,684 ft.) is the highest point in the eastern United States.

*****

Popular travel destinations in North Carolina are Charlotte, Raleigh, Asheville, Greensboro, Durham, and Wilmington. If you go to Asheville, visit the Biltmore House and Gardens with its 250 rooms, 33 bedrooms, 43 bathrooms, 65 fireplaces, and three kitchens. Also, go to Grove Park Inn for dining and a spectacular view of the mountain range. To me, there is no view more magnificent than the Blue Ridge Mountains during the fall foliage.

The Woolworth building in Greensboro is a significant landmark of the Civil Rights Movement. At 4 p.m. on February 1, 1960, four black freshmen from North Carolina A&T State University entered the store on North Elm Street and seated themselves in the "white-only" section of the lunch counter, launching the Greensboro sit-ins. The four young men were Ezell Blair, Jr., Franklin McCain, Joseph McNiel, and David Richmond.

NORTH DAKOTA

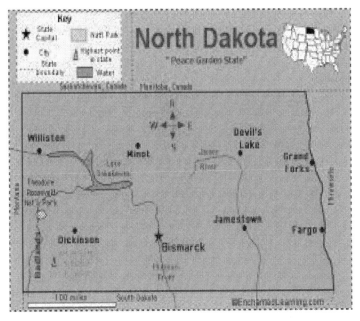

39th State / November 2, 1889 / Rank in area sq. miles: 19

Nickname: Peace Garden State

Capital: Bismarck

Most populous cities: Fargo, Bismarck, Grand Forks

Attractions: North Dakota Heritage Center, North Dakota State Capitol, in Bismarck; Bonanzaville, in

West Fargo; Ft. Union Trading Post National Historic Site; International Peace Garden, in Dunseith; Elkhorn Ranch site, in Theodore Roosevelt National Park; Ft. Abraham Lincoln State Park, in Mandan; Dakota Dinosaur Museum, in Dickinson; Knife River Indian Villages National Historic Site; Scandinavian Heritage Park, in Minden

Things to see and places to visit in the most populous states:

Fargo - North Dakota State University, Celebrity Walk of Fame, Maury Wills Museum*, World's Largest Baseball Bat - Big Bruce, Roger Maris Museum

Bismarck - State Capitol Building (tallest building in the state), North Dakota Heritage Center, Gateway to Science Center

Grand Forks - University of North Dakota, Center for Aerospace Sciences at the University of North Dakota

Well-known North Dakotans and residents:

Angie Dickinson - Film Actress, Television Actress (1931-)

Lawrence Welk - Conductor, Television Personality (1903-1992)

Peggy Lee - Film Actress, Singer, Songwriter, Television Actress (1920-2002)

Eric Sevareid - Actor, Writer, Journalist (1912-1992)

Interesting Information

- North Dakota grows more sunflowers than any other state.
- With a population of 5 people, Maza is the smallest city in North Dakota.
- North Dakota does not have towns or villages. Each place is officially a city, no matter how small it is.

- North Dakota is the least visited state in America.

- North Dakota State Capital; at 242 feet height, is the tallest building in the state and the third tallest capitol in the country.

- Rhode Island, the smallest state in the U.S., could fit inside North Dakota 46 times.

- North Dakota produces more honey than any other state.

- North Dakota has some of the world's best farmland.

- Most of the state is used for farming and ranching.

*****

My first trip to North Dakota was to visit my son, Kenneth Dimitri, who was stationed at Grand Forks AFB. Attractions in Grand Forks are the University of North Dakota, Japanese Gardens, and the North Dakota Museum of Art.

My second visit was to Fargo. I escorted a group of more than 40 people there so that they could say they had been to North Dakota. Several in the group laid claim that North Dakota was the fiftieth state they visited. What was most impressive to the group was that when we arrived in Fargo, there were amber waves of grain.

The Red River flows through Fargo, Moorehead, and Grand Forks in the United States and Winnipeg in Canada. Attractions in Fargo are Fargo Air Museum and the Fargodome, associated with the University of North Dakota.

If you go to Bismarck, you cannot miss the 19-story capitol Art Deco building downtown. It is the tallest building in the city.

OHIO

17th State / March 1, 1803 /Rank in area sq. miles: 34

Nickname: Buckeye State

Capital: Columbus

Most populous cities: Columbus, Cleveland, Cincinnati

Attractions: Hopewell Culture National Historic Park, in Chillicothe; Cuyahoga Valley National Park; Armstrong Air and Space Museum, in

Wapakoneta; National Museum of the U.S. Air Force, near Dayton; Pro Football Hall of Fame, First Ladies National Historic Site, in Canton; Cedar Point Amusement Park, in Mason; Lake Erie Islands, Cedar Point amusement park, in Sandusky; birthplaces, homes of, and memorials to presidents W.H. Harrison, Grant, Hayes, Garfield, B. Harrison, McKinley, Taft, and Harding; Amish Country, particularly in Holmes County; German Village historic neighborhood, Franklin Park Conservatory and Botanical Gardens, in Columbus; Rock and Roll Hall of Fame and Museum, West Side Market, Cleveland Metroparks Zoo, in Cleveland; Cincinnati Museum Center at Union Terminal; Toledo; Oberlin College, National Afro-American Museum and Cultural Center*, at Wilberforce University; Wilberforce University* (one of the oldest institutions of higher education for African Americans); Zoo, Harriet Beecher Stowe Cultural Resource Center, in Cincinnati; Paul Lawrence

206

Dunbar State Memorial*, in Dayton; Sojourner Truth Monument*, in Akron

Things to see and places to visit in the most populous cities:

Columbus - Columbus Zoo, The Topiary Garden, Ohio State House, The Ohio State University Campus, Columbus Zoo and Aquarium, the Short North, Franklin Park Conservatory and Botanical Gardens, Ohio Stadium, Martin Luther King, Jr. Center for the Performing and Cultural Arts*

Cleveland - Rock and Roll Hall of Fame and Museum, Cleveland Museum of Natural History, Great Lakes Science Center, James A. Garfield Monument, African American Museum*

Cincinnati - Cincinnati Museum Center, Music Hall, Fountain Square, Carew Tower and Observation Deck, American Sign Museum, Cincinnati Art Museum, Cincinnati Reds Hall of

Fame and Museum, National Underground Railroad Freedom Center*, Riverwalk, Stowe House

Well-known Ohioans and residents:

John Legend - Actor, Singer, Songwriter (1978-)

Russell Wilson - Football Player, Athlete (1988-)

Halle Berry - Film Actress (1966-)

LeBron James - Basketball Player (1984-)

Ruby Dee - Actress, Screenwriter, Poet, Playwright, Civil Rights Activist (1922-2014)

Nancy Wilson - Singer, Television Personality (1937-)

Dorothy Dandridge - Film Actress, Singer, Pin-Up (1922-1965)

Paul Warfield - Football Player, Athlete (1942-)

Toni Morrison - Writer (1931-)

Paul Lawrence Dunbar - Poet, Author (1872-1906)

Kathleen Battle - Singer (1948-)

Don King - Boxing Promoter (1931-)

Anita Baker - Singer, Songwriter (1958-)

Carl Stokes - News Anchor, Lawyer, Mayor (1927-1996)

Edwin Moses - Track and Field Athlete (1955-)

Granville T. Woods - Inventor (1856-1910)

John Heisman - Football Player, Coach, Athlete (1896-1936)

Don Shula - Coach (1930-)

George Steinbrenner - Business Leader (1930-2010)

Doris Day - Actress, Animal Rights Activist (1924-)

Jack Paar - Radio Talk Show Host, Television Talk Show Host (1918-2004)

Norman Vincent Peale - Academic, Minister, Journalist (1898-1993)

John D. Rockefeller, Jr. - Philanthropist (1874-1960)

Branch Rickey - Business Leader, Civil Rights Activist (1881-1965)

Sarah Jessica Parker - Film Actress, Theater Actress, Television Actress, Producer (1965-)

Drew Carey - Game Show Host, Television Actor, Comedian (1958-)

Paul Newman - Film Actor, Race Car Driver, Theater Actor, Television Actor (1925-2008)

Ted Turner - Philanthropist (1938-)

Cy Young - Baseball Player (1887-1955)

Dr. Mehmet Oz - Surgeon, Author, TV Talk Show Host (1946-)

Roy Rogers - Film Actor, Singer, Guitarist, Television Actor, Television Personality (1911-1998)

John Glenn - Astronaut, Military Leader, Pilot, U.S. Senator (1921-2016)

Thomas Edison - Inventor (1847-1931)

May Lin - Sculptor, Architect, Artist, Educator (1959-)

Edwin M. Stanton - Government Official, Civil Rights Activist, Lawyer (1814-1869)

Interesting Information

- The first ambulance service was established in Cincinnati in 1865.

- Cleveland boasts America's first traffic light. It was installed on August 5, 1914.

- Akron was the first city to use police cars.

- Cincinnati had the first professional city fire department.

- Akron is the rubber capital of the world.

- Cleveland is the home of the Rock and Roll Hall of Fame.

- Cleveland became the world's first city to be lit electrically in 1879.

- The Professional Football Hall of Fame is located in Canton.

- The first full-time automobile service station was opened in 1899 in Ohio.

- Oberlin College was founded in 1833. It was the first interracial and co-educational college in the United States.

- Paul Lawrence Dunbar of Dayton is known as the poet laureate of African Americans.
- Half of the presidents who died in office were from Ohio: William Harrison, James Garfield, William McKinley, and Warren G. Harding.
- Cleveland has the largest outdoor chandelier in the United States.

*****

Seven United States presidents were born in Ohio. Steubenville, Ohio, is the birthplace of Edwin McMasters Stanton, who served as Secretary of War under President Abraham Lincoln during the American Civil War. He was a civil rights activist, Supreme Court Justice, and a lawyer. Stanton School in Jacksonville, FL, where James Weldon Johnson attended and later served as principal, was named in his honor. When Lincoln was assassinated in 1865, Stanton was by Lincoln's bedside and is credited with the quote, "Now he is with the angels."

A number of people who resided in Ohio were associated with the movement to free slaves. The famed white abolitionist John Brown lived in a house in Akron. The Harriet Beecher Stowe Cultural Center is in Cincinnati. She used some of the stories in her book *Uncle Tom's Cabin* to persuade thousands of white Americans to become involved in the anti-slavery movement.

Sandusky, Ohio, is noted as an abolition center and an important stop on the Underground Railroad. Other Ohio cities along the Underground Railroad were Cincinnati, Toledo, Oberlin, and Cleveland.

Oberlin College, like Berea College in Kentucky, was one of the first accredited colleges in America to enroll Black students in the 1800s.

The National Afro-American Museum and Cultural Center is located at Wilberforce University. The college was also a site on the Underground Railroad.

OKLAHOMA

46th State / November 16, 1907 / Rank
in area sq. miles: 20

Nickname: Sooner State

Capital: Oklahoma City

Most populous cities: Oklahoma City, Tulsa,
Norman

Attractions: Cherokee Heritage Center, in
Tahlequah; Oklahoma City National Memorial and
Museum, National Cowboy and Western Heritage
Museum, White Water Bay and Frontier City

amusement parks, Museum of Osteology, Bricktown neighborhood, in Oklahoma City; Will Rogers Memorial Museums, Claremore and Oologah; Philbrook Museum of Art, Gilcrease Museum, in Tulsa; Price Tower Arts Center, in Bartlesville; Sam Noble Museum of Natural History; Seminole Nation Museum, in Wewoka

Things to see and places to visit in the most populous cities:

Oklahoma City - Oklahoma City National Memorial, National Cowboy and Western Heritage Museum, Museum of Osteology (only skeleton museum in the U.S.), State Capitol, Science Museum of Oklahoma, Omnidome, Oklahoma City University

Tulsa - Philbrook Museum of Art, University of Tulsa, Oklahoma Jazz Hall of Fame

Norman - University of Oklahoma, Legends Lobby at Barry Switzer Center, National Weather Center, Sam Noble Oklahoma Museum of Natural History

Well-known Oklahomans and residents:

Cornel West - Academic, Educator, Philosopher, Scholar, Civil Rights Activist (1953-)

John Hope Franklin - Historian, Journalist (1915-2009)

Ralph Ellison - Academic, Educator, Literary Critic, Author (1914-1994)

Will Rogers - Film Actor (1879-1935)

Wilma Mankiller - Women's Rights Activist (1945-2010)

Oral Roberts - Evangelist (1918-2009)

Ron Howard - Film Actor, Television Actor, Director, Producer, Television Personality (1954-)

Dr. Phil - Talk Show Host (1950-)

Sam Walton - Entrepreneur, Businessperson (1918-1992)

Garth Brooks - Singer, Guitarist, Songwriter (1962-)

Brad Pitt - Film Actor (1963-)

Jim Thorpe - Baseball Player, Basketball Player, Boxer, Football Player, Hockey Player, Track and Field Athlete (c.1888-1953)

Reba McEntire - Singer (1955-)

Mickey Mantle - Baseball Player (1931-1995)

Elizabeth Warren - Legal Professional, Government Official, U.S. Representative, U.S. Senator, Educator (1949-)

James Garner - Film Actor, Television Actor (1928-2014)

Carrie Underwood - Film Actress, Reality Television Star, Singer, Songwriter, Television Actress (1983-)

Troy Aikman - Football Player (1966-)

Gene Autry - Singer, Film Actor, Guitarist (1907-1998)

Johnny Bench - Baseball Player (1947-)

Tony Randall - Film Actor, Television Actor, Producer, Director (1920-2004)

Interesting Information

- The world's first parking meter was installed in Oklahoma City on July 16, 1935.
- There is an operating oil well on state capitol grounds called Capitol Site No. 1.
- The National Cowboy Hall of Fame is in Oklahoma.
- An Oklahoman, Sylvan Goldman, invented the first shopping cart.
- Oklahoma is one of only two states whose capital cities' names include the name, the other is Indianapolis, Indiana.
- Oklahoma has the largest Native American population of any state in the United States.

*****

Oklahoma City has the National Cowboy and Western Heritage Museum and Museum of Osteology. The Osteology Museum is America's only skeleton museum. The National Weather Center is in Norman.

The National Memorial Museum in Oklahoma City is probably one of the most stunning museums I have ever visited. It is a memorial to the people that were killed in the bombing of the Alfred P. Murrah Federal Building on April 19, 1995. The Outdoor Symbolic Memorial with the Field of Empty Chairs to represent the 168 killed and 19 smaller chairs represent the children killed in the bombing. It is an amazing transformation that will leave you with an unforgettable memory.

OREGON

33rd State / February 14, 1859 / Rank in area sq. miles: 9

Nickname: Beaver State

Capital: Salem

Most populous cities: Portland, Salem, Eugene

Attractions: Multnomah Falls, Columbia River Gorge; Timberline Lodge, Mount Hood National Forest; Crater Lake National Park; Oregon Dunes National Recreation Area; Ft. Clatsop (Lewis and Clark National Historical Park), Astoria Column, in

220

Astoria; Oregon Caves National Monument; International Rose Test Garden, Lan Su Chinese Garden, Pittock Mansion, Oregon Museum of Science and Industry, in Portland; High Desert Museum, in Bend; *Spruce Goose* (largest aircraft ever built), Evergreen Aviation and Space Museum, McMinnville; Oregon Coast Aquarium, in Newport

Things to see and places to visit in the most populous cities:

Portland - Washington Park, International Rose Test Garden, Portland Japanese Garden

Salem - Oregon State Capitol, Williamette University, Riverfront Park

Eugene - Jordan Schnitzer Museum of Art at the University of Oregon, Museum of Natural History and Culture at the University of Oregon, University of Oregon

Well-known Oregonians and residents:

Esperanza Spalding - Bassist, Singer, Musician (1984-)

Ashton Eaton - Track and Field Athlete (1988-)

Douglas C. Englebart - Inventor, Computer Programmer (1925-2013)

Kathleen Hanna - Women's Rights Activist, Singer (1968-)

Linus Pauling - Chemist, Scientist (1901-1994)

Beverly Cleary - Author (1916-)

Phil Knight - Business Magnate (1938-)

Interesting Information

- Oregon has more ghost towns than any other state.
- Oregon and New Jersey are the only two states without self-service gas stations.
- Eugene was the first city to have one-way streets.
- Portland is known as "The City of Roses."

- The Oregon Trail is the longest of the overland routes used in the westward expansion of the United States.

*****

The Museum of Natural and Cultural History and the Oregon Air and Space Museum are in Eugene. Eugene is heralded as "Tracktown U.S.A." Track and field began at the University of Oregon in 1895. Portland has beautiful rose gardens, so when you visit, be sure to stop and smell the roses; I did. You may want to travel the Oregon coastline. Mt. Hood at 11,239 feet is an unmistakable landmark with its snow-capped mountains.

I remember traveling through western Oregon en route to Seattle. It was a majestic view of nature. If you want to see green pastures, the serenity of nature undisturbed, winding rivers and more, travel to Oregon and see how Mother Nature embraces the state.

PENNSYLVANIA

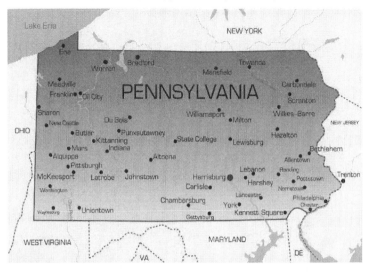

2nd State / December 12, 1787 / Rank in area sq. miles: 33

Nickname: Keystone State

Capital: Harrisburg

Most populous cities: Philadelphia, Pittsburgh, Allentown

Attractions: Liberty Bell Center at Independence National Historic Park, Franklin Institute, Philadelphia Museum of Art, in Philadelphia; Valley Forge National Historic Park, King of Prussia; Gettysburg National Military Park; Pennsylvania

Dutch Country, in Lancaster County; Hershey Park, in Hershey; Duquesne Incline, Carnegie Museums of Pittsburgh, Heinz Hall for the Performing Arts, in Pittsburgh; Pocono Mountains; Pine Creek Gorge (Pennsylvania Grand Canyon); Fallingwater (house designed by Frank Lloyd Wright); Steamtown National Historic Site, in Scranton; U.S. Brig *Niagara* Maritime Museum, Presque Isle State Park, in Erie; Longwood Gardens, in Kennett Square; Mother Bethel AME Church*, in Philadelphia; Intercultural Resource Center, in Gettysburg; Lincoln University* (one of the oldest institutions of higher education for African Americans), in Oxford; African American Historical and Cultural Museum*, Temple University - Charles L. Blockson Afro-American Collection, University of Pennsylvania - The University Museum of Archaeology/Anthropology, in Philadelphia; Thaddeus Stevens Tomb, in Lancaster

Things to see and places to visit in the most populous cities:

Philadelphia: Independence National Historic Park, Liberty Bell Pavilion, Independence Hall, Philadelphia Museum of Art, City Center, Franklin Institute Science Museum, Society Hill Historic District, African American Museum in Philadelphia*, National Constitution Center, The Academy of Natural Science of Drexel University, Betsy Ross House, Mother Bethel AME Church*, African-American Historical and Cultural Museum, Temple University - Charles L. Blockson Afro-American Collection, University of Pennsylvania - The University Museum of Archaeology/Anthropology

Pittsburgh - Carnegie Museum of Art, Carnegie Science Center, Point State Park, Mt. Washington Inclines, Nationality Classrooms at the Cathedral of Learning, University of Pittsburgh, Cathedral of Learning (42 floors) at the University of Pittsburgh

226

Allentown - America on Wheels Museum, Mack Trucks Historical Museum

Well-known Pennsylvanians and residents:

Marian Anderson - Diplomat, Singer (1897-1993)

Kevin Hart - Actor, Comedian (1979-)

Bill Cosby - Film Actor, Television Actor, Comedian, Television Producer (1937-)

Allan LeRoy Locke - Educator, Philosopher, Scholar, Journalist (1885-1954)

Will Smith - Actor, Rapper (1968-)

Guion S. Bluford - Astronaut, Pilot, Scientist (1942-)

Billie Holiday - Singer (1915-1959)

Richard Allen - Civil Rights Activist, Minister, Journalist (1760-1831)

Jill Scott - Singer (1972-)

Sherman Hemsley - Television Actor (1938-2012)

Kobe Bryant - Basketball Player (1978-)

August Wilson - Playwright (1945-2005)

Daniel Hale Williams - Surgeon (1856-1931)

Ethel Waters - Film Actress, Singer, Theater Actress, Television Actress (c.1896-1977)

Bayard Rustin - Civil Rights Activist (1912-1987)

Judith Jamison - Ballet Dancer, Choreographer (1943-)

Reggie Jackson - Baseball Player (1946-)

Billy Eckstine - Trumpet Player, Singer, Songwriter (1914-1993)

Wilt Chamberlain - Basketball Player (1936-1999)

Patti LaBelle - Film Actress, Singer (1944-)

Lee Daniels - Director, Producer (1959-)

Roy Campanella - Baseball Player (1921-1993)

Ed Bradley - News Anchor (1941-2006)

Viola Gregg Liuzzo - Civil Rights Activist (1925-1965)

Richard Gere - Civil Rights Activist, Anti-War Activist, Film Actor, Pianist, Theater Actor, Philanthropist (1949-)

Solomon Guggenheim - Philanthropist (1861-1949)

Lee Iacocca - Business Leader (1924-)

Grace Kelly - Film Actress, Princess of Monaco (1929-1982)

Dan Marino - Football Player, Athlete (1961-)

Margaret Mead - Anthropologist, Women's Rights Activist (1901-1978)

George C. Marshall - Government Official, General (1880-1959)

Joe Nameth - Football Player, Athlete (1943-)

Arnold Palmer - Golfer (1929-2016)

Robert Edwin Perry - Explorer (1856-1920)

Betsy Ross - Folk Hero (1752-1836)

Tommy Lasorda - Baseball Player, Coach (1927-)

Sharon Stone - Film Actress (1958-)

Joe Biden - U.S. Vice President, U.S. Representative (1942-)

Tina Fey - Film Actress, Theater Actress, Television Actress, Television Producer, Screenwriter, Comedian (1970-)

Benjamin Franklin - Writer, Inventor (1706-1790)

Mark Cuban - Businessman (1958-)

Taylor Swift - Singer (1989-)

Joe Montana - Football Player, Athlete (1956-)

Jimmy Stewart - Film Actor, Theater Actor (1908-1997)

Interesting Information

- In 1909 the first baseball stadium was built in Pittsburgh.
- Hershey is considered the Chocolate Capital of the United States.
- The world's largest chocolate and cocoa factory is in Hershey, PA.
- In 1913 the first automobile service station opened in Pittsburgh.

- In 1946 Philadelphia became the home of the first computer.

- The first daily newspaper was published in Philadelphia on September 21, 1784.

- Other firsts in Pennsylvania are as follows: The first oil field was drilled in the state; it had the first medical school, savings bank, television broadcast, and zoo in America.

*****

Philadelphia is one of America's most historical cities. Major attractions are Independence National Historic Park, Liberty Bell Pavilion, Independence Hall, Philadelphia Museum of Art (stairs became famous after they were used for the classic American *Rocky* films), City Center, and the Franklin Institute of Science Museum.

The Philadelphia Mint was the first official mint in the United States of America. At that time, 1792, Philadelphia was the nation's capital.

Also, Mother Bethel A.M.E. Church is in Philadelphia. It was founded by Richard Allen, who was named the first bishop, and the church became known as Mother Bethel. While leading the church, he and his wife, Sarah, established a station on the Underground Railroad, aiding escaped slaves seeking freedom in the north by hiding them in the basement of Mother Bethel. They are both buried in a tomb beneath the church.

If you are a history buff, Philadelphia is the city for you. In 1776, The Declaration of Independence was signed in Independence Hall. Other documents signed in the Hall are the Article of Confederation (1781) and the Constitution (1783).

RHODE ISLAND

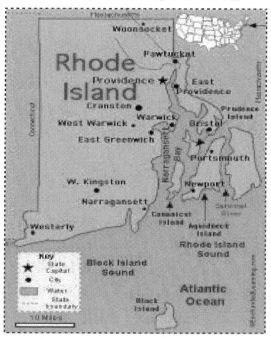

13th State / May 29, 1790 / Rank in area sq. miles: 50

Nickname: Little Rhody, Ocean State

Capital: Providence

Most populous cities: Providence, Warwick, Cranston

Attractions: Block Island; International Tennis Hall of Fame and Museum, in Newport; Rhode Island School of Design Museum of Art, Water Fire Art

233

Installation, in Providence; Slater Mill Historic Site, in Pawtucket; Gilbert Stuart Birthplace and Museum, in Saunderstown

Things to see and places to visit in the most populous cities:

Providence - Rhode Island School of Design, Brown University, Providence College, Roger Williams Park, State House, Water Place Park and Riverwalk, Culinary Arts Museum, Prospect Park

Cranston - Culinary Archives and Museum at Johnson and Whales University

Well-known Rhode Islanders and residents:

Meredith Vieira - Talk Show Host, News Anchor (1953-)

David Hartman - Talk Show Host (1935-)

Interesting Information

- Rhode Island is the smallest state in size. It covers an area of 1,214 square miles. Its distance from north to south is 48 miles and east to west 37 miles. It consists of 36 islands and has over 400 miles of coastline.

- Rhode Island was the last of the original thirteen colonies to become a state. It waited until people were sure the Bill of Rights would be added to the Constitution.
- Rhode Island is home to the first National Lawn Tennis Championship in 1899.
- The state is home to the first open golf tournament in 1895.
- Rhode Island has no county government. It is divided into 39 municipalities each having its own form of local government.
- The first circus in the United States was in Newport in 1774.

*****

I enjoyed visiting Providence. One reason may have been because my time was spent in the vibrant downtown area near the capitol. Rhode Island is a beautiful state.

A top attraction for me was the beautiful campus of Brown University where I learned about the Brown Curriculum. This "new curriculum" eliminated core requirements shared by Brown undergraduates and created specific departmental concentration requirements. This approach allows students to serve as the architects of their course of study. Students take a course for a grade of satisfactory or unrecorded - no credit. At the time we were admiring the campus, Dr. Ruth J. Simmons was president. She was the first African-American president of an Ivy League institution.

Other attractions are historic Federal Hill and Roger Williams Park Zoo. If you like tennis, stop by the International Tennis Hall of Fame in Newport.

The Rhode Island State House is a beautiful place. On a future visit I would like to walk in the rotunda and take a tour of the capitol.

SOUTH CAROLINA

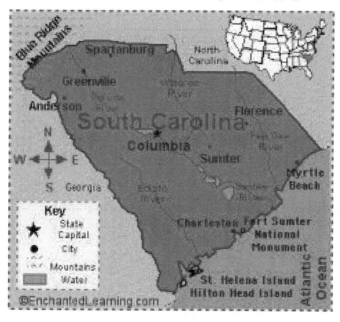

8th State / May 23, 1788 / Rank in sq. miles: 40

Nickname: Palmetto State

Capital: Columbia

Most populous cities: Columbia, Charleston, North Charleston

Attractions: Historic Charleston, Waterfront Park, Charleston Museum (est. 1773, oldest in the U.S.), Middleton Place, Magnolia Plantation and Gardens,

Drayton Hall, in Charleston; Ft. Sumter National Monument (where the first shots of the Civil War were fired), in Charleston Harbor; Cypress Gardens, in Moncks Corner; Boone Hall Plantation and Gardens, in Mt. Pleasant; Brookgreen Gardens, in Murrells Inlet; Myrtle Beach, Hilton Head Island; Andrew Jackson State Park, in Lancaster; South Carolina State Museum, Riverbanks Zoo, in Columbia; Penn Center Historic District*, in Frogmore; Robert Smalls House*, in Beaufort; Mary McLeod Bethune Birth Site Historical Marker*, in Mayesville; the Benjamin E. Mays Historic Site and Museum*, in Greenwood; Cultural Exchange Center*, in Greenville

Things to see and places to visit in the most populous cities:

Columbia - Riverbanks Zoo and Botanical Garden, University of South Carolina, South Carolina State House, Columbia Canal and Riverfront Park, South Carolina State Museum, EdVenture Children's

Museum, Trinity Episcopal Cathedral, Robert Mills House and Gardens, African American History Monument*, Allen University*, Benedict College*, Woodrow Wilson Family Home, Mann-Simons Cottage*

Charleston - Charleston Waterfront Park, Arthur Ravenel Jr. Bridge, Battery and White Point Gardens, College of Charleston, Cathedral of Saint John the Baptist, Charles Towne Landing, St. Michael's Church, South Carolina Aquarium, Charleston's Museum Mile on Meeting Street, Charleston City Market, Ft. Sumter National Historic Monument, Denmark Vesey House*, Avery Research Center for African-American History and Culture at the College of Charleston, Emanuel AME Church*

North Charleston - Riverfront Park, North Charleston and American LaFrance Fire Museum and Education Center

Well-known South Carolinians and residents:

Mary McLeod Bethune - Educator, Civil Rights Activist (1875-1955)

Benjamin E. Mays - Educator, Minister, Sociologist, Social Activist (1894-1984)

James E. Clyburn - U.S. Representative (1940-)

James Brown - Singer, Songwriter, Dancer, Activist, Musician (1933-2006)

Tim Scott - U.S. Representative, U. S. Senator (1965-)

Chris Rock - Film Actor, Theater Actor, Television Actor, Comedian, Director, Producer (1965-)

Kelly Miller - Mathematician (1863-1939)

Chadwick Boseman - Actor, Director, Screenwriter (1977-)

Chubby Checker - Singer (1941-)

Althea Gibson - Golfer, Tennis Player (1927-2003)

Viola Davis - Film Actress, Theater Actress (1965-)

Jesse Jackson - Civil Rights Activist, Minister, Journalist (1941-)

Hal Jackson - Business Leader, Disc Jockey (1915-2012)

William H. Johnson - Painter (1901-1970)

Robert Smalls - U.S. Representative, Pilot (1839-1925)

Eartha Kitt - Actress, Singer (1927-2008)

Ernest Everett Just - Educator, Biologist, Scientist (1883-1941)

Dizzy Gillespie - Trumpet Player, Singer, Songwriter (1917-1993)

Ronald E. McNair - Astronaut, Physicist (1950-1986)

Joe Frazier - Boxer (1944-2011)

Kevin Garnett - Basketball Player (1976-)

Darius Rucker - Singer, Songwriter (1966-)

Larry Doby - Baseball Player, Coach (1923-2003)

Marian Wright Edelman - Writer, Lawyer, Civil Rights Activist (1939-)

Alice Childress - Theater Actress, Playwright, Author (1916-1994)

Septima Poinsette Clark - Educator, Civil Rights Activist (1898-1987)

Charlayne Hunter-Gault - Radio Personality, News Anchor, Civil Rights Activist, Journalist (1942-)

Alonzo J. Ransier - Lt. Governor, U.S. Congressman (1834-1882)

Isaiah De Quincey Newman - Clergyman, Civil Rights Leader, State Senator (1911-1985)

Charles F. Bolden, Jr. - Astronaut, Military Leader (1946-)

Modjeska M. Simkins - Public Health Reform, Social Reformer, Civil Rights Activist (1899-1992)

Matthew J. Perry - Lawyer, U.S. Federal Judge (1921-2011)

John B. Watson - Academic, Psychologist (1878-1958)

Ernest F. Hollings - U.S. Senator, Governor (1922-)

William Westmoreland - General (1914-2005)

Andie MacDowell - Film Actress, Model (1958-)

John Edwards - U.S. Representative (1953-)

Leeza Gibbons - Talk Show Host, News Anchor, Television Producer (1957-)

Vanna White - Game Show Host (1957-)

Sarah Moore Grimké - Women's Activist, Civil Rights Activist (1792-1873)

Strom Thurmond - U.S. Senator, Governor (1902-2003)

Doc Blanchard - Football Player, Athlete (1924-2009)

Richard W. Riley - Governor (1933-)

Interesting Information

- The first battle of the Civil War took place at Fort Sumter.
- Johnston is known as the Peach Capital of the World.

- Duncan Park baseball stadium in Spartanburg is the oldest minor league stadium in the nation.

- Sumter has the largest Gingko farm in the world.

- South Carolina is the only state in the United States to own and operate its own school bus fleet.

- South Carolina is the only state in the U.S. that grows tea.

- South Carolina has some unique town names, including Welcome, Due West, Fountain Inn, Coward, Ninety Six, and South of the Border.

- South Carolina's Strom Thurmond was the first U.S. Senator ever elected by write-in votes, on November 2, 1954.

- The capital was moved from Charleston to Columbia in 1786.

- South Carolina was the first state to secede from the Union before the Civil War.

- More Revolutionary War battles were fought in South Carolina than in any other state.
- The first passenger train in the United States ran between Augusta, Georgia, and Charleston, South Carolina, in 1834.
- In 1862, the first Southern school for freed slaves was established in Frogmore, South Carolina.

*****

Myrtle Beach and Charleston are two of the most popular tourist destinations in the United States. Other South Carolina attractions include the State House, the African American History Monument, Riverbanks Zoo and Botanical Gardens, Brookgreen Garden, Cathedral of Saint John the Divine, Mother Bethel A.M.E. Church, and Pearl Fryar Topiary Garden.

Avery Research Center - College of Charleston for African-American and Culture is a part of the

College of Charleston. It is the country's largest research center devoted to the Gullah culture.

Mann-Simons Cottage is the only historic house in the Columbia area that was originally owned by African-Americans. Dr. Mary McLeod Bethune's birth site historical marker is in Mayesville. She founded Bethune-Cookman University in Daytona Beach, Florida, and directed its policies for thirty years.

Penn Center Historic District in Frogmore on St. Helena Island is the site of the former Penn School, one of the country's first schools for freed slaves. During the 1960s it played a role in the Civil Rights Movement by supporting school desegregation, voter registration, and training for community organizations in the South. Dr. Martin Luther King, Jr., and his staff held meetings at the conference center which was used for Peace Corp volunteer training.

The Benjamin E. Mays Historic Site and Museum is in Greenwood. You will experience how African-American sharecroppers lived and understand the monumental rise of Dr. Mays from son of former enslaved parents to president of Morehouse College in Atlanta, GA. Dr. Mays was awarded more than 56 honorary degrees, published nearly 2,000 articles, and wrote nine books.

On January 31, 1961, students from Friendship Junior College and others in Rock Hill picked the McCrory's on Main Street to protest the segregated lunch counters at the business. A historical marker and a restaurant are at the location. Friendship Nine memorabilia is available at the restaurant.

For more information on South Carolina sites, see the *Green Book of South Carolina: A Travel Guide to S.C. African American Cultural Sites*, released by the South Carolina African American Heritage Commission.

SOUTH DAKOTA

40th State / November 2, 1889 / Rank in area sq. miles: 17

Nickname: Coyote State, Mount Rushmore State

Capital: Pierre

Most populous cities: Sioux Falls, Rapid City, Aberdeen

Attractions: Mt. Rushmore National Memorial, in Keystone; Harney Peak (tallest east of the Rockies); Custer State Park; Crazy Horse Memorial (mtn. carving in progress); Wind Cave National Park, near Hot Springs; Black Hills National Forest; Needles Highway, part of Peter Norbeck National Scenic

Byway; Minuteman Missile National Historic Site; Deadwood (1876 gold rush town); Jewel Cave National Monument, near Custer; Badlands National Park; Great Lakes of South Dakota; Great Plains Zoo and Delbridge Museum of Natural History, in Sioux Falls; Corn Palace, in Mitchell; Reptile Gardens, Chapel in the Hills Bear Country USA, in Rapid City

Things to see and places to visit in the most populous cities:

Sioux Falls - St. Joseph Cathedral, Veterans Memorial Park, Michaelangelo's David replica, Sioux Empire Medical Museum, The South Dakota Battleship Museum, Falls Park

Rapid City - South Dakota Air and Space Museum, Museum of Geology, Dinosaur Park, Berlin Wall Exhibit, Museum of the American Bison, Mount Rushmore National Memorial, a pow pow, Journey Museum

Aberdeen - Decotah Prairie Museum, South Dakota State University

Well-known South Dakotans and residents:

Sitting Bull - Warrior, Military Leader (1831-1890)

Crazy Horse - Folk Hero, Warrior, Military Leader (c.1842-1877)

George McGovern - U. S. Senator (1922-2012)

Hubert H. Humphrey - Academic, Mayor, U.S. Representative, U.S. Senator (1911-1978)

Tom Brokaw - News Anchor, Journalist (1940-)

Sparky Anderson - Coach (1934-2010)

Ernest O. Lawrence - Educator, Inventor, Physicist, Scientist (1901-1958)

Bob Barker - Television Game Show Host (1923-)

Mary Hart - Television Personality (1950-)

Russell Means - Activist (1939-2012)

Cheryl Ladd - Film Actress, Singer, Author (1951-)

Interesting Information

- Mount Rushmore is the world's greatest mountain carving. It has the faces of George Washington, Thomas Jefferson, Theodore Roosevelt, and Abraham Lincoln. The carving took 14 years to complete.

- Mitchell is the home of the world's only Corn Palace, built with 3,500 bushels of ear corn.

- The largest buffalo herd in the U.S. lives at Standing Butte Ranch near Pierre.

- The largest working gold mine in the Americas is in South Dakota.

*****

Mount Rushmore is the sculpture of the heads of four former United States Presidents carved into the granite on the southeast side of Mount Rushmore.

Attractions in Rapid City are Main Street Square, City of President Statues, and South Dakota Air and Space Museum. Custer State Park, the Badlands, and the Black Hills are also in South Dakota.

TENNESSEE

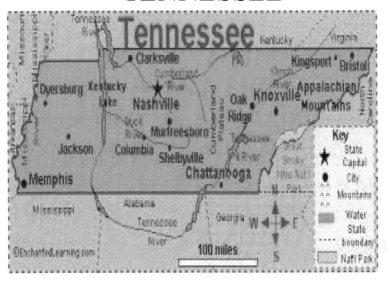

16th State / June 1, 1796 / Rank in

area sq. miles: 36

Nickname: Volunteer State

Capital: Nashville

Most populous cities: Memphis, Nashville,

Knoxville

Attractions: Lookout Mountain, Tennessee Aquarium, Ruby Falls, in Chattanooga; Great Smoky National Park; Lost Sea (largest underground lake in the U.S.), in Sweetwater; Cherokee National Forest; Cumberland Gap National Historical Park;

252

James K. Polk Ancestral Home, in Columbia; American Museum of Science and Energy, Oak Ridge; The Hermitage (home of President Andrew Jackson); Country Music Hall of Fame and Museum, Ryman Auditorium, Belle Meade Plantation, Parthenon replica, Grand Ole Opry, in Nashville; Dollywood theme park, in Pigeon Forge; Graceland (home of Elvis Presley), Sun Studio, in Memphis; Alex Haley Museum and Interpretive Center*, in Henning; Casey Jones Village, in Jackson; Afro-American Museum*, in Chattanooga,

Things to see and places to visit in the most populous cities:

Memphis - National Civil Rights Museum*, the Lorraine Motel Complex*, Graceland, Stax Museum of American Soul Music*, Slave Haven/Buckle Estate Museum, Beale Street, Peabody Ducks, Sun Studios, Pink Palace Museum

Nashville - Country Music Hall of Fame and Museum, Opryland Hotel Gardens, The Hermitage, Home of President Andrew Jackson, The Parthenon, Jubilee Hall, Fisk University*

Knoxville - University of Tennessee, McClung Museum of Natural History and Culture, World's Fair Park, Sunsphere Tower, Women's Basketball Hall of Fame, Alex Haley Heritage Square*, Beck Cultural Exchange Center*, University of Tennessee Football Hall of Fame

Well-known Tennesseans and residents:

Mary Styles Harris - Scientist (1949-)

Julian Bond - Government Official, Educator, Civil Rights Activist (1940-2015)

Morgan Freeman - Film Actor, Theater Actor, Television Actor, Producer (1937-)

Tina Turner - Singer (1939-)

Wilma Rudolph - Track and Field Athlete (1940-1994)

Aretha Franklin - Singer (1942-)

Thomas "Hitman" Hearns - Boxer (1958-)

Oscar Robinson - Basketball Player (1938-)

Benjamin Hooks - Civil Rights Activist, Lawyer, Judge, Minister (1925-2010)

Nikki Giovanni - Poet, Writer, Educator, Civil Rights Activist (1943-)

Isaac Hayes - Actor, Singer (1942-2008)

Bobby "Blue" Bland - Singer (1930-2013)

Usher - Singer, Television Actor (1978-)

Mary Church Terrell - Women's Rights Activist, Civil Rights Activist, Educator (1863-1954)

Bessie Smith - Blues Singer (1894-1937)

Sam Rayburn - U. S. Representative (1882-1961)

Justin Timberlake - Film Actor, Singer (1981-)

Jack Hanna - Zoologist, Scientist, Philanthropist, Television Personality, Journalist (1947-)

Tennessee Ernie Ford - Singer (1919-1991)

Dixie Carter - Television Actress (1939-2010)

Cybill Shepherd - Film Actress, Model, Television Actress (1950-)

George Hamilton - Film Actor, Talk Show Host, Television Actor (1939-)

Kenny Chesney - Singer, Songwriter (1968-)

Dinah Shore - Singer, Television Personality (1916-1994)

Dolly Parton - Singer, Songwriter (1946-)

Bill Belichick - Coach (1952-)

Miley Cyrus - Film Actress, Singer, Television Actress (1992-)

Alvin C. York - Warrior, Military Leader (1887-1964)

Interesting Information

- Tennessee has more than 3,800 documented caves.

- Bristol is known as the birthplace of country music.

- Tennessee is bordered by eight states (so is Missouri). On a clear day, seven states are visible from Lookout Mountain, near Chattanooga.

- Coca-Cola was first bottled in 1899 at a plant in downtown Chattanooga.

- The Alex Haley boyhood home in Henning is the first stated-owned historic site devoted to African Americans.

- Tennessee was the last state to secede from the Union during the Civil War and the first to be readmitted after the war.

- The nation's oldest African-American architectural firm, McKissack and McKissack, is located in Nashville.

- The nation's oldest African-American financial institution, Citizens Savings Bank and Trust Company, is located in Nashville.

- Cumberland University, located in Lebanon, lost a football game to Georgia Tech on October 7, 1916 by a score of 222-0. The Georgia Tech coach was George Heisman for whom the Heisman Trophy is named.

It was at Knoxville College, where I met the great college choir director Dr. Nathan Carter. The college is now closed, but he later went on to become director of the renowned Morgan State University choir in Baltimore. My stay in Knoxville enabled me to develop a likeness for mountains, particularly the Great Smoky Mountains near Knoxville. The Great Smoky Mountain National Park is the country's most visited national park.

The Beck Cultural and Exchange Center, dedicated to the history and achievement of black people in eastern Tennessee, is in Knoxville. The mansion was originally the home of James and Ethel Beck. Of all the thoroughfares that run through black communities in the United States, none is probably more celebrated in song and story than Beale Street. A statue of W. C. Handy, trumpet in hand, looks down on the street from a park near

Third Street. The view is from the house where he lived.

The Lorraine Motel, now the National Civil Rights Museum, is where Dr. Martin Luther King, Jr. was assassinated on April 4, 1968. Fisk University in Nashville established itself as a preeminent university associated with a number of Black scholars who studied or taught at the university. Included are social philosopher, W.E.B. Du Bois; sociologist, E. Franklin Frazier; historian, John Hope Franklin; Congressmen, William L. Dawson and Charles Drew; Solicitor General of the United States, Wade H. McCree; jurist, Constance Baker Motley; poets James Weldon Johnson, Arna Bontemps, Sterling Brown, and Nikki Giovanni; tenor Roland Hayes; and novelist John O. Killens. Some of the historic buildings are the Administration Building, the Fisk Chapel, and Jubilee Hall.

Alex Haley Museum and boyhood home is in Henning, Tennessee. He was born in Ithaca, NY, but grew up in Henning. The late author listened to his ancestors tell the history of their ancestors; as a result, he published *Roots*.

The Opryland Hotel and Gardens, and the Grand Ole Opry House are in Nashville.

TEXAS

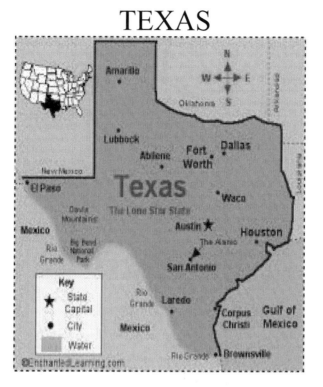

28th State / December 29, 1845 / Rank in area
sq. miles: 2

Nickname: Lone Star State

Capital: Austin

Most populous cities: Houston, San Antonio,
Dallas, Austin

Attractions: Fort Davis National Historic Site; Six
Flags Over Texas, in Arlington; SeaWorld San

Antonio, Six Flags Fiesta Texas, The Alamo, San Antonio, San Antonio Missions National Historical Park, San Antonio River Walk, in San Antonio; National Cowgirl Museum and Hall of Fame, Kimbrell Art Museum, Ft. Worth Zoo, Bureau of Engraving and Printing, in Ft. Worth; Lyndon B. Johnson National Historical Park, in Johnson City; LBJ Presidential Library and Museum, Bullock Texas State History Museum, in Austin; George Bush Presidential Library and Museum, in College Station; Dallas Arboretum and Botanical Garden, Sixth Floor Museum at Dealey Plaza, George W. Bush Presidential Library and Museum, in Dallas; *USS Lexington,* Texas State Aquarium, Padre Island National Seashore, in Corpus Christi

Things to see and places to visit in the most populous cities:

Houston - Space Center Museum, Houston Museum of Natural Science, Museum of Fine Arts, The

Health Museum, Gerald D. Hines Waterfall Park, Rice University Campus, Holocaust Museum

San Antonio - River Walk, The Alamo, San Antonio River (boat ride), St. Joseph Catholic Church, Institute of Texas Culture, Tower of the Americas, Cathedral of San Fernando (oldest in the U.S.), Japanese Tea Garden

Dallas - Pioneer Plaza, Dealey Plaza, Natural History Museum, The Sixth Floor Museum, Dallas Arboretum and Botanical Gardens, The George W. Bush Presidential Library and Museum, Perot Museum of Nature and Science, Southern Methodist University, Dealey Plaza National Historic Landmark District, African American Museum*, Museum of African-American Life and Culture*

Austin - State Capitol, University of Texas, LBJ Presidential Library, George Washington Carver Museum*

Well-known Texans and residents:

Michael Strahan - Talk Show Host, Football Player, Athlete (1971-)

Ernie Banks - Baseball Player, Coach (1931-2015)

Bessie Coleman - Pilot (1892-1926)

Beyonce Knowles - Film Actress, Singer (1981-)

Barry White - Singer, Music Producer (1944-2003)

Johnny Mathis - Singer (1935-)

Rafer Johnson - Track and Field Athlete (1935-)

James Farmer - Civil Rights Activist, Journalist (1920-1999)

Chandra Wilson - Film Actress, Theater Actress, Television Actress (1969-)

Phylicia Rashad - Film Actress, Theater Actress, Television Actress (1948-)

Billy Preston - Pianist (1946-2006)

Bobby Seale - Civil Rights Activist (1936-)

Frank Robinson - Baseball Player (1935-)

Barbara Jordan - Civil Rights Activist, U.S. Representative (1936-1996)

Scott Joplin - Pianist, Songwriter (c.1868-1917)

Michael Johnson - Track and Field Athlete (1967-)

Jack Johnson - Boxer (1878-1946)

George Foreman - Boxer, Minister (1949-)

Tom Bradley - Law Enforcement, Lawyer, Mayor (1917-1998)

Alvin Ailey - Choreographer (1931-1989)

Debbie Allen - Film Actress, Theater Actress, Television Actress, Choreographer (1950-)

Percy Julian - Civil Rights Activist, Lawyer (1920-2009)

Forest Whitaker - Film Actor, Filmmaker (1961-)

Charles Brown - Singer, Pianist (1922-1999)

Willie Brown - Mayor (1934-)

Maynard Jackson - Lawyer, Mayor (1938-2003)

Joe Morgan - Baseball Player (1943-)

C. Wright Mills - Sociologist, Activist, Journalist (1916-1962)

Bob Schieffer - News Anchor (1937-)

Melinda Gates - Business Leader, Philanthropist (1964-)

Carol Burnett - Actress, Comedian (1933-)

Tom Landry - Coach (1924-2000)

Mary Martin - Film Actress, Singer, Theater Actress, Television Actress (1913-1990)

Dan Rather - News Anchor (1931-)

Gene Autry - Film Actor, Singer, Guitarist, Television Actor (1907-1998)

Tanya Tucker - Reality Television Star, Singer (1958-)

Sissy Spacek - Film Actress, Television Actress (1949-)

Chesley Sullenberger - Pilot (1951-)

Dwight D. Eisenhower - General, Journalist, U. S. President (1890-1969)

Willie Nelson - Animal Rights Activist, Singer, Songwriter (1933-)

Kenny Rogers - Singer, Songwriter (1938-)

Lyndon B. Johnson - U.S President, U.S. Vice President, U.S. Representative (1908-1973)

Audie Murphy - Actor (1925-1971)

Howard Hughes - Producer, Director, Investor, Inventor, Aviator (1905-1976)

Debbie Reynolds - Film Actress, Singer (1932-2016)

Jaclyn Smith - Film Actress, Television Actress (1945-)

Joan Crawford - Film Actress, Theater Actress, Dancer, Pin-up (1905-1977)

Tommy Lee Jones - Film Actor, Television Actor, Director (1946-)

Barbara Mandrell - Singer (1948-)

Jennifer Garner - Film Actress, Theater Actress, Television Actress (1972-)

Larry Hagman - Theater Actor, Television Actor, Television Producer (1931-2012)

Interesting Information

- Austin is the largest capital of all of the states.
- The word Texas, an Indian word, means "friend."
- Texas is the largest of the contiguous 48 states.
- Texas has more counties than any other state (254).
- Of the nation's largest cities, three are in Texas: Houston, Dallas, and San Antonio.
- The state extends 801 miles from north to south and 773 miles from east to west.
- The only state larger than Texas is Alaska.
- The Dallas-Ft. Worth Airport is larger than New York City's Manhattan Island.
- Texas is larger than all of New England, NY, PA, OH and IL combined.
- Port Arthur is closer to Jacksonville, FL on the Atlantic than it is to El Paso. El Paso is closer to Needles, CA, than it is to Dallas.

- Dr. Pepper was invented in Waco in 1885.

- Texas has the most farms of any state.

- The phrase "Don't mess with Texas" originated 30 years ago as the slogan for a campaign meant to combat littering.

*****

To say Texas is big is more than a cliché. Attractions in Texas include San Antonio River Walk; Texas State Capitol in Austin; the Alamo in San Antonio; LBJ Presidential Library in Austin; and the Sixth Floor Museum/School Book Depository where shots were fired and killed President John F. Kennedy on November 22, 1963, as he was riding in a motorcade.

In the LBJ Presidential Library and Museum, you will be surprised at the number of pens (72) LBJ used to sign the Civil Rights Act into law in 1964. One of the crown jewels of the archives is the taped telephone recording of LBJ doing the business of his presidency. You can pick up a handset and hear LBJ talking to Dr. Martin Luther King, Jr. about civil rights.

The University of Texas in Austin has one of the largest undergraduate enrollments in the nation. According to *U.S. News* data in 2014, the University of Central Florida in Orlando had the largest undergraduate enrollment in the nation with 52,532.

Juneteenth (also called Freedom Day or Emancipation Day) celebrates the emancipation of the last remaining slaves in the USA, celebrated on June 19th. Although the Civil War ended on April 9, 1865, news of the victory of the Union Army and the enforcement of the freeing of all slaves did not reach outlying areas of the USA for months.

UTAH

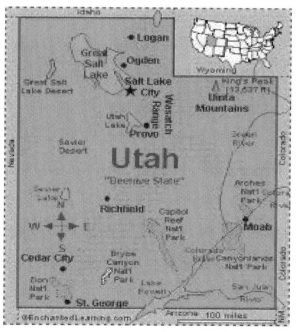

45th State / January 4, 1896 / Rank in area sq. miles: 13

Nickname: Beehive State

Capital: Salt Lake City

Most populous cities: Salt Lake City, West Valley City, Provo

Attractions: Temple Square (site of Mormon Church headquarters), in Salt Lake City; Great Salt Lake; Zion, Canyonlands, Bryce Canyon, Arches, and Capitol Reef national parks; Dinosaur, Rainbow

271

Bridge, Timpanogos Cave, and Natural Bridges natural monuments; Lake Powell; Flaming Gorge National Recreation Area; Utah Olympic Park, Sundance Film Festival, in Park City

Things to see and places to visit in the most populous cities:

Salt Lake City - Temple Square, Mormon Temple, State Capitol, Mormon Tabernacle, This is the Place Heritage Park, University of Utah, Great Salt Lake

Provo - Brigham Young University, BYU Earth Science Museum, BYU Museum of Paleontology, The Soap Factory, Crandell Historical Printing Museum

Well-known Utahans and residents:

Wallace Henry Thurman - Literary Critic, Playwright, Author, Editor (1902-1934)

Donny Osmond - Game Show Host, Talk Show Host, Singer, Music Producer, Television Actor, Journalist (1957-)

Marie Osmond - Singer, Theater Actress, Television Personality (1959-)

Loretta Young - Actress (1913-2000)

J. Willard Marriott - Restaurant and Hotel Entrepreneur (1900-1985)

James Wood - Film Actor, Television Actor (1947-)

Interesting Information

- The Mormon Temple in Salt Lake City took 40 years to complete.

- Utah is the only state whose capital's name is made up of three words.

- All three words in Salt Lake City have four letters each.

- The federal government owns 65% of the state's land.

- Utah has the highest literacy rate in the nation.

*****

Utah has several natural attractions along with Zion National Park and Bryce Canyon National

Park. I found the Mormon Temple and the Family History Library in Salt Lake City interesting attractions. The Great Salt Lake, the largest inland lake west of the Mississippi, is in Salt Lake City.

VERMONT

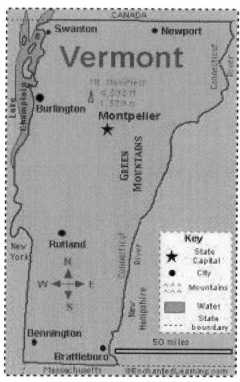

14th State / March 4, 1791 / Rank in area sq. miles: 45

Nickname: Green Mountain State

Capital: Montpelier

Most populous cities: Burlington, Essex, South Burlington

Attractions: Shelburne Museum; Shelburne Farms; Vermont Marble Museum, in Proctor; Bennington

Battle Museum; President Calvin Collidge Homestead, in Plymouth; Ben and Jerry's Factory, in Waterbury; Stowe, Killington, and Burke ski resorts; Hildene (Robert Todd Lincoln home), in Manchester; Marsh-Billings-Rockefeller National Historical Park, in Woodstock; William Lloyd Garrison Marker, Bennington Museum

Things to see and places to visit in the most populous cities:

Burlington - University of Vermont, World's Tallest Filing Cabinet, Ben and Jerry's Ice Cream Factory

Well-known Vermonters and residents:

Chester A. Arthur - Lawyer, U.S. Vice President, President (1829-1886)

Brigham Young - Missionary (1801-1877)

Joseph Smith - Religious Figure (1805-1844)

Rudy Vallee - Singer, Radio Talk Show Host (1901-1986)

Jody Williams - Educator, Philanthropist (1950-)

Stephen A. Douglas - U.S. Representative (1813-1861)

John Dewey - Academic, Educator, Philosopher (1859-1952)

Interesting Information

- Vermont was the first state admitted to the Union after the ratification of the Constitution.

- With a population fewer than 9,000 people, Montpelier, Vermont, is the smallest capital in the U.S.

- Montpelier is the largest producer of maple syrup in the U.S.

- Vermont's largest employer isn't Ben and Jerry's; its IBM.

- Vermont's state capitol building is one of only a few to have a gold dome.

*****

Vermont is the Green Mountain State and was the first state to outlaw slavery. It is known for its maple syrup, its maple sugar, and its excellent skiing. Attractions include the State House (Montpelier), University of Vermont (Burlington), Church Street Marketplace (Burlington), Morse Farm Sugarworks (Montpelier), and Ben & Jerry's Ice Cream Factory (Waterbury). I enjoyed visiting the maple sugarworks and eating Ben & Jerry's ice cream.

VIRGINIA

10th State / June 25, 1788 /Rank in area sq. miles: 35

Nickname: Old Dominion

Capital: Richmond

Most populous cities: Virginia Beach, Norfolk, Chesapeake, Richmond

Attractions: Colonial Williamsburg, Busch Gardens Williamsburg, Jamestown Settlement in Williamsburg; Yorktown Victory Center; Wolf Trap National Park for the Performing Arts, near Vienna; Arlington National Cemetery; George Washington's Mount Vernon; Thomas Jefferson's Monticello, in Charlottesville; Stratford Hall (Robert E. Lee's birthplace); Appomattox Court House National Historical Park; Shenandoah National Park; Blue Ridge National Parkway; Virginia Beach; Kings Dominion amusement park, in Doswell; Charles Richard Drew House*, in Arlington; Booker T. Washington National Monument*, east of Rocky Mount on VA Route 122; Benjamin Banneker Boundary Stone*, in Arlington

Things to see and places to visit in the most populous cities:

Virginia Beach - The Virginia Beach Boardwalk, Virginia Beach Oceanfront, Virginia Science Museum

Norfolk - MacArthur Memorial, Chrysler Museum of Art, Navy Station Norfolk

Chesapeake - Chesapeake Planetarium

Richmond - Capital Square, Edgar Allen Poe Museum, Maggie Walker House*, Virginia State House, St. John's Episcopal Church (where Patrick Henry spoke the line "Give me Liberty or Give me Death"), Black History Museum Cultural Center of Virginia*, Capitol Square, Federal Reserve Money Museum, Maggie Lena Walker National Historic Site*

Well-known Virginians and residents:

Pharrell Williams - Music Producer, Singer, Musician (1973-)

Booker T. Washington - Educator, Civil Rights Activist (1856-1915)

Henry "Box" Brown - Civil Rights Activist, Magician (1856-1879)

Bill "Bojangles" Robinson - Film Actor, Dancer (1878-1949)

Michael Vick - Football Player, Athlete (1980-)

281

Mildred Loving - Civil Rights Activist (1939-2008)

Vernon Johns - Civil Rights Activist, Pastor (1892-1965)

Carter G. Woodson - Historian (1875-1950)

Chris Brown - Singer, Dancer (1989-)

Sally Hemings - Enslaved woman of mixed race owned by President Thomas Jefferson (c.1773-1835)

Ella Fitzgerald - Singer (1917-1996)

Charles S. Johnson - Sociologist (1893-1956)

Henrietta Lacks - African American whose cells advanced scientific research and sparked debate over medical ethics (1920-1951)

Gabby Douglas - Gymnast, Athlete (1955-)

Wanda Sykes - Comedian (1964-)

Ruth Brown - Singer, Theater Actress (1928-2006)

Jesse L. Martin - Film Actor, Theater Actor, Television Actor (1969-)

Dred Scott - Civil Rights Activist (c.1795-1858)

Martin Robison Delany - Doctor, Civil Rights Activist, Author, Editor (1812-1885)

Ella Baker - Civil Rights Activist (1903-1986)

Pearl Bailey - Film Actress, Singer, Theater Actress, Television Actress, Journalist (1918-1990)

Arthur Ashe - Tennis Player, Activist (1943-1993)

James Armistead - Warrior, Spy, Military (c.1748-1830)

Clara Brown - Philanthropist (c.1800-1885)

Dorothy Height - Women's Rights Activist, Civil Rights Activist (1912-2010)

Douglas Wilder - Governor, Mayor (1931-)

Allen Iverson - Basketball Player (1975-)

Blanche K. Bruce - U.S. Representative (1841-1898)

Nat Turner - Revolutionist (c.1800-1831)

Warren Beatty - Film Actor, Director (1937-)

Willard Scott - Television Personality (1934-)

Ed Schultz - Radio Talk Show Host (1954-)

Pocahontas - Folk Hero (c.1595-1617)

Sandra Bullock - Film Actress (1964-)

Katie Couric - Talk Show Host, News Anchor (1957-)

Patrick Henry - U.S. Representative, U.S. Governor (1736-1799)

Shirley MacLaine - Film Actress, Singer, Theater Actress, Television Actress, Dancer, Journalist (1934-)

Woodrow Wilson - Educator, U.S. President (1856-1924)

Thomas Jefferson - Diplomat, Government Official, U.S. Vice President, U.S. President (1743-1826)

George Washington - General, U.S. President (1732-1799)

Walter Reed - Medical Professional, Doctor, Scientist (1851-1902)

John Marshall - Supreme Court Justice (1755-1835)

Interesting Information

- Virginia is known as "the birthplace of the nation."

- Jamestown was the first settlement.

- Eight U.S. presidents were born in Virginia: Washington, Jefferson, Madison, Monroe, Harrison, Tyler, Taylor, Wilson.

- Seven U.S. presidents are buried in Virginia: Washington, Jefferson, Madison, Monroe, Tyler, Taft, Kennedy.

- The Pentagon building in Arlington is the largest office building in the world.

- The first peanuts grown in the United States were grown in Virginia.

- Richmond was also the capital of the Confederate States during the Civil War.

- The first Thanksgiving in North America was held in Virginia in 1619.

*****

Some attractions in Virginia are Appomattox Court House National Historic Park, Mt. Vernon, Colonial Williamsburg, Arlington National Cemetery, the Pentagon, Booker T. Washington National Monument (near Rocky Mount), and the Maggie Lena Walker House in Richmond.

Hampton (Institute) University, Booker T. Washington's alma mater, opened in 1868 and had a large settlement of slaves. As early as 1861, slaves fled to Hampton seeking protection within the Union army lines.

When he was 15 years old, John "Box" Brown, a noted abolitionist speaker, was sent to Richmond. His escape from slavery on March 29, 1849, was one of the most sensational ever recorded in fugitive slave accounts. With the help of others, he was shipped in a box from Richmond to Philadelphia. It was a journey of 27 hours. The late historian, John Hope Franklin, wrote a classic book, *From Slavery*

286

to Freedom. Brown gave new meaning to the phrase from slavery to freedom with his creative escape. He was a symbol of the Underground Railroad Movement.

WASHINGTON

42nd State / November 11, 1889 / Rank in area sq. miles: 18

Nickname: Evergreen State

Capital: Olympia

Most populous cities: Seattle, Spokane, Tacoma

Attractions: Seattle Center, Space Needle, EMP Museum, Museum of Flight, Pike Place Market, Underground Tour, in Seattle; Mount Rainier, Olympic, and North Cascades national parks; Mount St. Helens; National Volcanic Monument; Puget

Sound; San Juan Islands; Grand Coulee Dam; Columbia River Gorge; National Scenic Area; Riverfront Park, in Spokane; Snoqualmie Falls

Things to see and places to visit in the most populous cities:

Seattle - Space Needle, Pike Place Market, Museum of Flight, Boeing Factory, University of Washington, International Fountain, Sky View Observatory, The Underground Tour, Olympic Sculpture Park, Seattle Waterfront, Dr. Martin Luther King, Jr. Memorial*

Spokane - Riverfront Park, Clock Tower, Gonzaga University, Cathedral of Our Lady of Lourdes, St. John's Cathedral

Tacoma - Museum of Glass, Tacoma Art Museum, Union Station

Well-known Washingtonians and residents:

Jimi Hendrix - Singer, Guitarist, Songwriter (1962-1970)

Gail Devers - Track and Field Athlete (1966-)

Craig Nelson - Film Actor, Television Actor, Television Personality (1944-)

Bing Crosby - Film Actor, Singer, Songwriter (1903-1977)

John Elway - Football Player, Athlete (1960-)

Carol Channing - Theater Actress (1921-)

Kenny G - Saxophonist (1956-)

Bob Barker - Animal Rights Activist, Game Show Host (1923-)

Adam West - Film Actor, Television Actor (1928-)

Bill Gates - American Business Magnate, Investor, Philanthropist, Author (1955-)

Interesting Information

- The state of Washington is the only state to be named after a United States president.
- Seattle is the home of the first revolving restaurant, which opened in 1961.
- Washington state produces more apples than any other state in the Union.

- Washington state's capitol building was the last state capitol to be built with a rotunda.

- Microsoft Corporation is located in Redmond.

- The oldest operating gas station in the United States is in Zillah.

- The world's largest building by volume - Boeing's assembly factory in Everett - spans 98.3 acres and 472 million cubic feet. Seventy-five football fields could fit inside.

*****

You may want to be sleepless when you go to Seattle to see the attractions, and two of the most popular are Pike Place Market and the Space Needle. The 605 feet tall Space Needle was built for the 1962 World's Fair. You can see the city, the Puget Sound, and Mt. Rainier from atop the Space Needle. On a clear day the view is spectacular!

One of my favorite attractions is the University of Washington at Seattle. The campus is situated on the shores of Union and Portage bays, with views of the Cascade Range to the east and Olympic Mountains to the west. The campus Quad is beautiful!

WEST VIRGINIA

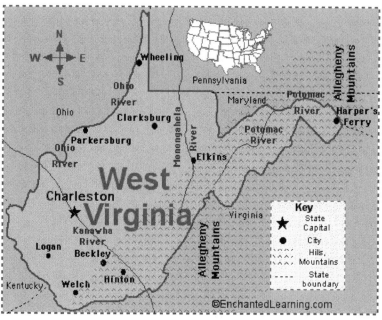

35th State / June 20, 1863 / Rank in area sq. miles: 41

Nickname: Mountain State

Capital: Charleston

Most populous cities: Charleston, Huntington, Parkersburg, Morgantown

Attractions: Harpers Ferry Historical National Park, Appalachian Trail Conservancy and Visitor Center, in Harpers Ferry; Clay Center for the Arts and Sciences and Avampato Discovery Museum, in

Charleston; The Greenbrier Resort, White Sulphur Springs; Berkeley Springs State Park; Seneca Rocks State Park; New River Gorge National River; Beckley Exhibition Coal Mine; Monongahela National Forest; Fenton Art Glass Company, in Williamston; Mountain State Forest Festival, in Elkins; Mountain State Art & Craft Fair, in Ripley; National Radio Astronomy Observatory in Green Bank (with world's largest fully steerable radio telescope); Cass Scenic Railroad State Park; Harpers Ferry National Historic Site*

Charleston - State Capitol, Heritage Towers*

Huntington - Museum of Radio and Technology, Huntington Museum of Art

Morgantown - West Virginia University, Earl L. Core Arboretum

Well-known West Virginians and residents:
Bill Withers - Singer, Songwriter (1938-)

Steve Harvey - Radio Personality, Writer, Film Actor, Game Show Host, Television Actor, Radio Talk Show Host (1957-)

Henry Gates - Academic, Educator, Historian, Scholar, Literary Critic, Filmmaker, Editor (1950-)

Don Knotts - Film Actor, Television Actor, Comedian (1924-2006)

Jerry West - Basketball Player, Coach (1938-)

Mary Lou Retton - Gymnast, Athlete (1968-)

Robert Graetz - Civil Rights Activist, Pastor (1928-)

Pearl Buck - Civil Rights Activist, Women's Rights Activist, Author (1892-1973)

Walter Reuther - Business Leader, Civil Rights Activist (1907-1970)

Chuck Yeager - Military Leader, Pilot (1923-)

Brad Paisley - Singer, Songwriter (1972-)

Interesting Information

- West Virginia is considered the southernmost Northern state and the northern most Southern state.

- Mother's Day was first observed at Andrews Church in Grafton on May 10, 1908.

- West Virginia has the oldest population of any state. The median age is 40.

- The first state sales tax in the United States went into effect in West Virginia on July 1, 1921.

- The first federal prison exclusively for women in the United States was opened in 1926 in West Virginia.

- Nearly 75% of West Virginia is covered by forest.

- Fifteen percent of the nation's total coal production comes from West Virginia.

- The first free delivery rural mail delivery was started in Charles Town on October 6, 1896, and then spread throughout the United States.

- The first brick street in the world was laid in Charleston on October 23, 1870, on Summers Street, between Kanawha and Virginia streets.

*****

Harpers Ferry Historical National Park, West Virginia State Museum, State Capitol, and West Virginia State University in Morgantown are some of the state's main attractions.

John Brown was a militant abolitionist known for his raid on Harpers Ferry in 1859. He worked with the Underground Railroad and used violent means to end slavery. On October 16, 1859, Brown led a party of 21 men on a raid of the federal armory of Harpers Ferry in Virginia (now West Virginia), holding dozens of men hostage with the plan of inspiring a slave insurrection. Many of Brown's men were killed, including two of his sons, and he was captured. On November 2, he was sentenced to death and executed. I visited the John Brown site in Harpers Ferry.

WISCONSIN

30th State / May 29, 1848 / Rank in area sq. miles: 23

Nickname: Badger State

Capital: Madison

Most populous cities: Milwaukee, Madison, Green Bay

Attractions: Wade House, in Greenbush; Villa Louis, in Prairie du Chien; Circus World Museum, in Baraboo; Wisconsin Dells; Old World Wisconsin, in Eagle; shoreline and state parks of Door County; House on the Rock, Taliesin, in Spring Green; Monjona Terrace Community and Convention Center, in Madison; Milwaukee Art Museum, Pabst Mansion, in Milwaukee

Things to see and places to visit in the most populous cities:

Milwaukee - Milwaukee's Lovely Lakefront, The Milwaukee Art Museum, The Greek Orthodox Church, Discovery World, Milwaukee City Hall, America's Black Holocaust Museum*, Wisconsin Black Historical Society Museum*

Madison - Wisconsin State Capitol, Monona Terrace, Olbrich Botanical Gardens, Arboretum and Geology Museum, Wisconsin Veterans Museum, Capital Square, University of Wisconsin

Green Bay - Lambeau Field, National Railroad Museum, Green Bay Packer Hall of Fame, Green

Bay Botanical Garden, Heritage Hill State Historical Park

Well-known Wisconsinites and residents:

Al Jarreau - Singer, Songwriter, Theater Actor, Television Actor (1940-2017)

John Ridley - Screenwriter (1965-)

Donald K. "Deke" Slayton - Astronaut (1924-1993)

Orson Welles - Film Actor, Director (1915-1985)

Harry Houdini - Magician (1874-1926)

Tom Snyder - News Anchor, Radio Talk Show Host (1936-2007)

Charlotte Rae - Actress, Singer (1926-)

Spencer Tracey - Film Actor, Theater Actor (1900-1967)

Don Ameche - Film Actor, Television Actor (1908-1993)

Gene Wilder - Actor, Comedian, Author (1933-2016)

Thornton Wilder - Playwright, Author (1897-1975)

Curley Lambeau - Football Player, Coach (1898-1965)

Interesting Information

- The first practical typewriter was designed in Milwaukee in 1867.

- Wausau is the Ginseng Capital of the World.

- Wisconsin is the Dairy Capital of the United States.

- The Republican Party was founded in Ripon in 1854.

- Green Bay is the Toilet Paper Capital of the World.

*****

Lambeau Field in Green Bay may be an attraction for Packer fans, but for others there is the Wisconsin State Capitol, Capitol Square, and the University of Wisconsin. A lot of events take place in Capitol Square. The University of Wisconsin lies along the southern shore of Lake Mendota in the city of Madison. Its fight song is "On, Wisconsin!" The Wisconsin Dells is a top attraction for tourists.

WYOMING

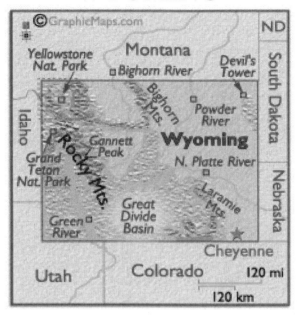

44th State / July 10, 1890 / Rank in area sq. miles:
10

Nickname: Equality State, Cowboy State

Capital: Cheyenne

Most populous cities: Cheyenne, Casper, Laramie

Attractions: Yellowstone National Park (est. 1872, first U.S. national park), Grand Teton National Park, National Elk Refuge, in Jackson; Devils Tower National Monument, Ft. Laramie National Historic

Site, Oregon Trail ruts, in Guernsey; Buffalo Bill Historical Center, in Cody; Cheyenne Frontier Days

Things to see and places to visit in the most populous cities:

Cheyenne - The Rodeo, Wyoming State Capitol, Cheyenne Depot Museum, Cheyenne Depot Plaza, Terry Bison Ranch, Cheyenne Gunslingers

Casper - American Heritage Center, University of Wyoming Anthropology Museum, University of Wyoming Art Museum, University of Wyoming Geological Museum

Laramie - University of Wyoming, University of Wyoming Geological Museum, University of Wyoming Art Museum

Well-known Wyomingites and residents:
　　Vernon J. Baker - Military Leader (1919-2010)
　　Jackson Pollock - Painter (1912-1956)

Jim Bullock - Film Actor, Theater Actor, Television Actor, Comedian, Television Personality (1955-)

Interesting Information

- Wyoming was the first state to give women the right to vote.
- The largest coal mine in the U.S. is Black Thunder located near Wright.
- The JC Penney store was started in Kemmerer.
- Very few people live on the plains and mountains of Wyoming.
- Wyoming has the lowest population of all 50 United States.

*****

For some reason, I enjoy riding on the plains of Wyoming. You can travel for miles and miles, and see much of nothing. Cheyenne, Wyoming's capital city, embodies the spirit of the Old West. It is considered the nation's rodeo and railroad capital.

Cheyenne's Frontier Days is the world's largest outdoor rodeo and Western celebration. Free pancake (three) breakfasts are served Monday, Wednesday, and Friday during Frontier Week from 7 am - 9 am at the Depot Plaza. We interacted briefly with the cowboys during Frontier Days on a stop in Cheyenne.

Of course, Yellowstone National Park is Wyoming's top tourist attraction with Old Faithful.

WASHINGTON, D.C.

July 16, 1790 / Rank in area sq. miles: 9

Nickname: Nation's Capital,
Federal City, "D.C."

Attractions: Capitol Building, Washington Monument, The White House, Smithsonian National Air and Space Museum, Kennedy Center, National Zoo, Lincoln Memorial, Vietnam Veterans Memorial, Thomas Jefferson Memorial, National Cathedral, Arlington National Cemetery, African American Civil War Memorial and Museum*,

308

Martin Luther King, Jr. National Memorial*, National Museum of African Art*, Korean War Veterans Memorial, Franklin Delano Roosevelt Memorial, Ford's Theater, World War II Memorial, Iwo Jima Memorial, Embassy Row, Mary McLeod Bethune Council National Historic Site*, Blanche K. Bruce House*, Ralph Bunche House*, Frederick Douglass National Historic Site*, Metropolitan African Methodist Church*, Mary Church Terrell House*, Carter G. Woodson House*, Howard University*

Well-known Washingtonians (DC) and residents:

Corey Booker - Mayor, U.S. Senator (1969-)

Euphemia Lofton Haynes - Mathematician (1890-1980)

Johnny Gill - Singer (1966-)

Taraji Henson - Film Actress, Television Actress (1970-)

Elgin Baylor - Business Leader, Basketball Player, Coach (1934-)

Charles Houston - Educator, Civil Rights Activist, Lawyer (1895-1950)

Benjamin O. Davis, Sr. - General (1877-1970)

Fannie Coppin - Missionary, Educator (c.1837-1913)

Sterling Brown - Educator, Literary Critic, Poet, Editor (1901-1989)

Frederick Douglass Patterson - Educator (1901-1983)

Jean Toomer - Poet, Playwright, Author (1894-1967)

Connie Chung - News Anchor, Journalist 1946-)

Helen Hayes - Actress (1900-1993)

Queen Noor of Jordan - Queen (1951-)

Robert Kennedy, Jr. - Environmental Activist, Lawyer, Radio Talk Show Host (1954-)

John F. Kennedy, Jr. - Publisher (1960-1999)

Interesting Information

- The only state in the United States that has fewer people than Washington, DC is Wyoming.

- DC residents pay taxes to the federal government, but they do not have a voting representative in Congress.

- While the city of Washington, DC was named after George Washington, the District was named in memory of Christopher Columbus.

- The *White House* was originally called the "President's Palace" or the "President's House."

- The Washington Monument (555 ft.) is the tallest object in DC.

- The White House features 6 levels, 412 doors, 147 windows, 28 fireplaces, 8 staircases, 3 elevators, and 35 different bathrooms.

- The MLK Jr. Memorial was made in China.

- George Washington never lived in the White House. It was completed a year after he died.

- The Library of Congress has 535 miles of bookshelves.

- Abraham Lincoln was the first American president to be assassinated (April 14, 1865).

*****

The fall of 2016, the National Museum of African American History and Culture - the newest museum of the Smithsonian Institution - opened. It is a place visitors can learn about the entire African-American experience that is inextricably woven into the fabric of America's history - from unimaginable horrors like slavery to inspiring triumphs like the election of the first black President.

The Museum brings history to life through the state-of-the-art interactive galleries and an unmatched collection of historical and cultural objects. The Museum serves as a beacon of learning, inspiration and remembrance that brings Americans together to reflect upon our shared history and culture.

United States Superlatives

The following is information I have categorized as United States extremes, which includes the biggest, smallest, highest, longest, first, most populous, etc. I think this information will be interesting as you travel, and you can use it for trivia, games, and quizzes.

****

First state: Delaware, which became a state on December 7, 1787

Most recent state: Hawaii, admitted August 21, 1959

Most populous state: California, 33,871,648 people (2000 U.S. Census Bureau)

Least populous state: Wyoming, 493,782 people (2000 U.S. Census Bureau)

Biggest City in the USA: New York, New York, with over 8,000,000 million people

States with the most bordering states: <u>Missouri</u> with 8 bordering states (Arkansas, Illinois, Iowa, Kansas, Kentucky, Nebraska, Oklahoma, Tennessee) and <u>Tennessee</u> with 8 bordering states (Alabama, Arkansas, Georgia, Kentucky, Mississippi, Missouri, North Carolina, Virginia)

Largest city by area: Yakutat, Alaska (Aout's Geography Guide).

Largest city area in the contiguous 48 states: Jacksonville, FL

Five Longest Highways in America

1. US 50: Ocean City, MD - West Sacramento, CA (3,011 miles)
2. US 30: Atlantic City, NJ - Astoria, OR (3,073 miles)
3. I - 90: Boston, MA - Seattle, WA (3,101 miles)

4. US 6: Provincetown, MA - Bishop, CA (3,207 miles)

5. US 20: Boston, MA - Newport, OR (3,365 miles)

10 Longest Interstate Highways

1. I - 90: Seattle, WA - Boston, MA (3,101.77 miles)

2. I - 80: San Francisco, CA - Teaneck, NJ (2,899.54 miles)

3. I - 40: Barstow, CA - Wilmington, NC (2,555.10 miles)

4. I - 10: Santa Monica, CA - Jacksonville, FL (2,460.34 miles)

5. I - 70: Baltimore, MD - Cove Ft., Utah (2,153.13 miles)

6. I - 95: Houlton, ME - Miami, FL (1,925.74 miles)

7. I - 75: Naples, FL - Sault Ste. Marie, Huron, MI (1,786.47 miles)

8. I - 94: Billings, MT - Port Huron, MI (1,585.20 miles)

9. I - 35: Laredo, TX - Duluth, MN (1,578.38 miles)

10. I - 20: Kent, TX - Florence, SC (1,539.38 miles)

Note: Total mileage of the Interstate system is 46,837 (2004). Interstate routes with odd-numbers run north-south. Routes with even numbers run east-west.

****

US Route 20 is America's longest highway, stretching from Boston, MA to Newport, OR. It runs through twelve states. Colfax Avenue is the longest street in America (26.8 miles). It is the main street that runs east-west through Denver, CO - Aurora, CO Metropolitan area.

Interstate I-95 was the most expensive route to build, costing $8 billion dollars. It goes through the largest number of states, 16. The only state without interstate routes is Alaska. The Interstate Highway System connects 45 of the 50 state capitals, including the nation's capital, Washington, DC.

Nicknamed the Mother Road and stretching for 2,448 miles from Chicago, Illinois, to Santa Monica, California, Route 66 might be the most celebrated road in American history. Though it is no longer a formal national highway, many of the towns, businesses, and attractions that sprung up along Route 66 during its mid-20th-century heyday are still thriving and offer today's travelers a chance to get their kicks along the historic highway. Adrain, Texas, is considered by many to be the midway point of Route 66 between Chicago and Los Angeles.

Tallest Buildings in the United States

1. One World Trade Center, New York, NY Height: 1,776 ft. Floors: 104

2. Willis Tower, Chicago, IL Height: 1,451 ft. Floors: 110

3. Trump International Hotel and Tower, Chicago, IL Height: 1,389 ft. Floors: 92

4. Empire State Building, New York, NY Height: 1,250 ft. Floors: 102

5. Bank of America Tower, New York, NY Height: 1,200 ft. Floors: 55

6. AON Building, Chicago, IL Height: 1,136 ft. Floors: 83

7. John Hancock Center, Chicago, IL Height: 1,127 ft. Floors: 100

8. Chrysler Building, New York, NY Height: 1,046 ft. Floors: 77

9. New York Times Building, New York, NY Height: 721 ft. Floors: 52

10. BOA Plaza, Atlanta, GA   Height: 1,023 ft. Floors: 55

11. U.S. Bank Tower, Los Angeles, CA Height: 1018 ft.   Floors: 73

12. J P Morgan Chase Tower, Houston, TX Height: 1,002 ft.   Floors: 75

While the World Trade Center in New York is a monument in some respects, the Gateway Arch (630 ft.), located in St. Louis, MO, is the tallest monument in the United States.

Most Popular Travel Destinations in the United States

1. New York, NY	2. Chicago, IL
3. San Francisco, CA	4. Las Vegas, NV
5. New Orleans, LA	6. Los Angeles, CA
7. San Diego, CA	8. Seattle, WA
9. Washington, DC	10. Orlando, FL
11. Honolulu, HI	12. Houston, TX
13. Charleston, SC	14. Boston, MA
15. Portland, OR	16. San Antonio, TX
17. Palm Springs, CA	18. Austin, TX
19. Branson, MO	20. Atlanta, GA
21. Phoenix, AZ	22. Myrtle Beach, SC
23. Saint Louis, MO	24. Nashville, TN
25. Miami Beach, FL	
Source: *Business Insider* (2014)	

2017 U.S. News Best Places To Live In The U.S.

1. Austin, TX	2. Denver, CO
3. San Jose, CA	4. Washington, DC
5. Fayetteville, AR	6. Seattle, WA
7. Raleigh-Durham, NC	8. Boston, MA
9. Des Moines, IA	10. Salt Lake City, UT
11. Colorado Springs, CO	12. Boise, ID
13. Nashville, TN	14. Charlotte, NC
15. Dallas-Fort Worth, TX	16. San Francisco, CA
17. Minneapolis-St. Paul, MN	18. Madison, WI
19. Grand Rapids, MI	20. Houston, TX

Most Visited Cities in the United States by Foreign Visitors

1. New York, NY	2. Los Angeles, CA
3. Miami, FL	4. San Francisco, CA
5. Las Vegas, NV	6. Orlando, FL
7. Washington, DC	8. Honolulu, HI
9. Boston, MA	10. Chicago, IL
Source: travelguy88 (2013)	

The Longest Main-Stem Rivers of the United States

1. Missouri River	2,341 miles
2. Mississippi River	2,202 miles
3. Yukon River	1,979 miles
4. Rio Grande River	1,759 miles
5. Arkansas River	1,469 miles
6. Colorado River	1,450 miles
7. Columbia River	1,243 miles
8. Red River	1,125 miles
9. Snake River	1,040 miles
10. Ohio River	979 miles

Longest U.S. Suspension Bridges

Name & Location	Feet
Verrazano-Narrows Lower NY Bay	4,260
Golden Gate Bridge San Francisco Bay	4,200
Mackinac Mackinac Straits, MI	3,800
George Washington Hudson River, NYC	3,500
Tacoma-Narrows Puget Sound at Tacoma, WA	2,800
Bronx-Whitestone East River, NYC	2,300
Delaware Memorial Delaware River, Wilmington, DE	2,150
Seaway Skyway, St. Lawrence River, Ogdensburg, NY	2,150
San Francisco-Oakland San Francisco Bay	2,047
Lake Pontchartrain Causeway in New Orleans, LA, is the longest bridge (23.83 miles) over water.	

Top Natural Attractions in the United States

1. The Grand Canyon (AZ)

2. Niagara Falls (NY)

3. Old Faithful at Yellowstone National Park (Wyoming)

4. Denali, AK (highest peak in North America)

5. Monument Valley (where the states of Utah and Arizona converge)

6. Devil's Tower (Wyoming Prairie)

Ten Highest Points in the United States

State	Peak	Elev-Ft Range (Level 3)
Alaska	Mount Denali	20,320 Alaska Range
California	Mount Whitney	14,495 Sierra Nevada
Colorado	Mount Elbert	14,443 Southern Rocky Mountains
Washington	Mount Rainier	14,411 Cascade Range
Wyoming	Mount Gannett Peak	13,804 Greater Yellowstone Rockies
Hawaii	Mauna Kea	13,796 Hawaii
Utah	Kings Peak	13,528 Western Rocky Mountains
New Mexico	Wheeler Peak	13,161 Southern Rocky Mountains
Nevada	Boundary Peak	13,140 Great Basin Ranges
Montana	Granite Peak	12,799 Greater Yellowstone Rockies

Mt. Mitchell in North Carolina is the tallest point (6,684 ft.) east of the Mississippi River. It is in the Blue Ridge Mountains.

The Underground Railroad

In about 1831 in Kentucky, a runaway slave named Trice escaped with his master chasing right behind. Trice got as far as the Ohio River, which separated the slave states from the free states. He jumped into the river, swam across, and disappeared. On this far side was Ohio and freedom.

His master, following in a boat, could not find him. The story is that the master said Trice "must have gone off (on) an underground railroad." Thus, the Underground Railroad is the name given to secret routes taken from the South to Freedom in the North. It was a name given to the network of people who hid and guided slaves as they followed the North Star to Canada. Agents were people who helped the fugitives; conductors were people who led them from one place to another; and stations were places to hide.

The National Park Service, Department of Interior, which printed *Taking the Train to Freedom* gave the following account of the Underground Railroad. The Underground Railroad originated during the Colonial era as slaves sought ways to escape the inhumane treatment of bondage.

Neither "underground" nor a "railroad," this secretive system was not initially organized but arose when escaped slaves sought refuge in unclaimed territories and newly settled colonies. With the assistance of agents such as the Quakers, free blacks, and Native Americans, bondsmen were able to gain their freedom. The efforts of the "underground" promoted the enactment of local fugitive slave laws, which were a response to the growing concerns of slaveholders who had lost numerous servants. As the nation continued to struggle over the morality of slavery, the invention of the cotton gin, in 1793, accorded the South justifications to perpetuate slavery because it was viewed essential to its economy.

The abolition movement of the early 1800s set its goal to exterminate slavery. To do so, abolitionists turned the "underground" into a well-organized system. Through the use of secret codes, "stations," "conductors," and "railways," runaway slaves, guided by the North Star, usually travelled to their destinations by night either alone or in small groups. Their plans did not entail standard routes since it was necessary to prevent capture; thus waterways, back roads, swamps, forests, mountains, and fields were used to escape. While in flight, slaves hid in barns, caves, cellars, boxes, wagons, and aboard ships. Food and shelter were provided at "stations" which were maintained by noted "conductors" such as William Still, Levi Coffin, and Frederick Douglass. Moreover, Presbyterian, African Methodist Episcopal, African Methodist Episcopal Zion, and the United Methodist churches gave refuge to escapees. Once runaways achieved their freedom, a few like Harriet Tubman, known as "Moses" to her people, returned to assist fellow slaves and loved ones to liberty. Single-handedly, Tubman made 19 trips to the South and led more than 300 slaves out of bondage.

By the 1850s, anti-slavery sentiment had reached its peak, and the "underground" program was challenged by slaveholders through a revised Fugitive Slave Act. This law called for the return of runaways and jeopardized the status of freedmen, especially those who resided in Northern states. Therefore, escape routes thus were no longer limited to Northern, Midwestern regions, and the federal territories of the United States. More than 100,000 American slaves sought freedom in these areas as well as Canada, Mexico, and the Caribbean. The Underground Railroad remained active until the end of the Civil War, as black bondsmen continued to use the system to flee the horrors of slavery.

From a travel standpoint, if you visit the Niagara area, then you can visit Harriet Tubman's church and hear her story. You will also learn about Anthony Burns, the slave at the root of the Boston riots in 1850 who later preached at the Baptist Church in St. Catharines. You can actually visit a former safe house where people would enter the basement by a tunnel from the river.

Uncle Tom's Cabin is located in Dresden, Ontario. Harriet Beecher Stowe immortalized the former slave, Josiah Henson. Henson, an abolitionist, activist, author, and minister, was born in Maryland but escaped to Upper Canada. It is believed he inspired the character of the fugitive slave, George Harris, in Stowe's *Uncle Tom's Cabin* (1852). He developed an African Canadian community.

The North American Black Historical Museum and Cultural Center is located in Amherstburg, Ontario, and contains many fascinating artifacts related to slavery, as well as pioneer implements built by the former slaves in Canada.

The John Walls Historic Site in Windsor is a fascinating trip back to a log cabin which was a terminal of the Underground Railway. This unique attraction takes you from Africa to America to Canada in a highly informative way. These historic Underground Railroad sites are near Detroit, MI.

Interesting information I learned was about the escape of Henry "Box" Brown, a slave in Virginia who was shipped in a box from Richmond, VA, to Philadelphia, PA, to freedom. His story will inspire you, and I encourage you to read his biography and narratives.

Underground Railroad Chronology

1607   Jamestown, Virginia, was settled by English colonists.

1619   Twenty Africans were shipped to Jamestown, Virginia, on Dutch ships.

1641   Massachusetts colony legalized slavery.

1660   Virginia colony legalized slavery.

1776   The Quakers declared that they will not own slaves.

1777   Northern states abolished slavery.

1793   Upper Canada's first Legislature passed a law prohibiting the introduction of more slaves and making any person born of a slave free upon reaching the age of 25.

1793   The first Fugitive Slave Law was passed in the United States providing for the return of runaway slaves. This fueled the birth of the "Underground Railroad."

1808   The United States Congress passed a law prohibiting importation of slaves.

1827   Levi Coffin, a Quaker and a leading "stationmaster," began assisting freedom seekers in Cincinnati, Ohio.

1833   Upper Canada refused to extradite fugitive slaves, Thornton and Lucie Blackburn, the principals in a mob rescue in Detroit, back to the U.S.

1833   The Emancipation Act abolished slavery throughout the British Empire. Canada was viewed as a safe haven for runaway slaves from the United States.

1838   Prompted by the case involving Jesse Happy, a fugitive slave who had escaped to

Canada, the British Government concluded that a slave extradition request from the United States must show evidence that the person committed a crime recognized in Canada. Therefore, slavery, and escape were not recognized in Canada.

1838　The Underground Railroad was "formally organized." Black abolitionist, Robert Purvis, became chairman of the General Vigilance Committee and "president" of the Underground Railroad.

1850　The Second Fugitive Slave Law passed in the United States resulted in a flood of slaves and free Blacks fleeing to the safety of Canada.

1851　Harriet Tubman moved to St. Catharines; it became the center of her anti-slavery activities for the next seven years.

1852   Harriet Beecher Stowe's *Uncle Tom's Cabin* is published as a response to the pro-slavery argument.

1857   The Supreme Court declared in Scott v. Sandford that Blacks are not U.S. citizens, and slaveholders have the right to seize slaves in free areas of the country.

<u>1861</u>   The Civil War begins.

<u>1863</u>   President Lincoln issued the Emancipation Proclamation, which declares "all persons held as slaves within any state … be in rebellion against the United States shall be then … forever free."

<u>1865</u>   The Civil War ends. The Thirteenth Amendment was amended to the U.S. Constitution and abolished slavery permanently.

Sources

- Cantor, George (1991). *Historic Black Landmarks A Traveler's Guide*. Detroit: Visible Ink Press.

- Curtis, Nancy C. (1996). *Black Heritage Sites The North - The South*: New York: The New Press.

- Ross, Wilma (1991). *Fabulous Facts About The 50 States*. New York: Scholastic Inc.

- Rozett, Louise, Editor (1991). *Fast Facts About States*. New York: Children's Press.

- Savage, Beth L., Editor (1994). *African American Historic Places*. New York: Preservation Press.

- Schultz, Patricia (2011). *1,000 Places To See Before You Die*. New York: Workman Publishing.

- Jansen, Sarah, Senior Editor (2015). *The World Almanac and Book of Facts*. New York: World Almanac Books.

CANADA

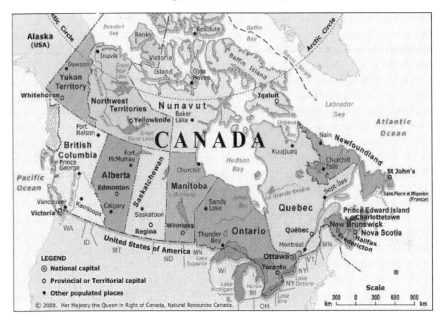

Most populous cities: Toronto (Ont.), Montreal (Que.), Vancouver (B.C.)

Attractions: Niagara Falls, Toronto's CN Tower, Old Quebec (Vieux-Quebec), Ottawa's Parliament Hill, St. John's Hill National Historic Site, Old Montreal, Victoria's Inner Harbor, Vancouver's Stanley Park, Canadian Museum for Human Rights, in Winnipeg, Canada is the second largest country, surpassed only by the Russian Federation. The

338

country is encased by the world's longest coastline. Distances in Canada can be vast. Consider the Trans-Canada Highway between Victoria (BC) and St. John's (NF), which at 4,860 miles long, is longer than the distance from London to Bombay. More than 50 percent of Canada's land is blanketed with rich forest ranges, accounting for 10 percent of the world's remaining forests and 20 percent of the world's wilderness areas.

Canada is made up of ten provinces and three territories. The provinces from east to west are British Columbia, Alberta, Saskatchewan, Manitoba, Ontario, Quebec, New Brunswick, Prince Edward Island, Nova Scotia, and further east, the province Newfoundland and Labrador. The territories are Yukon, the Northwest Territories (NWT), and Nunavut, Canada's newest territory, formed in 1999 out of the eastern part of the NWT and the homeland of the native Inuit. Ontario is larger than all other provinces except Ottawa.

There are some two million lakes in Canada, covering about 7.6% of the Canadian landmass. Canada shares four of the five Great Lakes, the sources of much of the fresh water in the world, with the United States. The largest lake situated entirely in Canada is Great Bear Lake in the Northwest Territories.

Canada has six time zones. The easternmost in Newfoundland is three hours 30 minutes behind Greenwich Mean Time (GMT). The other time zones are Atlantic, Eastern, Central, Rocky Mountain, and farthest west, the Pacific, which is eight hours behind GMT.

Canada Facts

- *Canada* is an Iroquoian language word meaning "village."
- Queen Elizabeth II of England is also the queen of Canada. Canada is part of the British Commonwealth.

- The governing body of Canada is called Parliament. They have a House of Commons (295) and a Senate (104). The Prime Minister is head of government and is much like our president.

- The Royal Canadian Mounted Police (Mounties) are the national police force. (They claim they always get their man.)

- The two main languages spoken in Canada are English and French.

- Canada shares the longest border in the world with the United States, totaling 5,525 miles (8891 kilometers).

- The most popular sport in Canada is ice hockey.

- Winnie the Pooh was based on a Canadian bear.

- West Edmonton Mall is the largest in North America. There are over 800 different stores and 23,000 employees. Twenty thousand vehicles can park in its lots.

- Basketball did not originate in Canada, but the man who invented it was a Canadian living in Massachusetts, James Naismith.
- Canada is the world's most educated country, over half of its residents have college degrees.
- Canada has more lakes than the rest of the world's lakes combined.
- In Newfoundland, the Atlantic Ocean sometimes freezes, so people play ice hockey on it.
- Being 1,178 miles (1,896 km), The Yonge Street in Canada is the longest street in the world.
- The Mall of America is owned by Canadians.
- Police Departments in Canada give out "positive tickets" when they see people doing something positive.

- Canada has the third largest oil reserves of any country in the world after Saudi Arabia and Venezuela.

- Anyone in Canada can send a letter to a member of Parliament (while it is in session) without paying postage.

- Life expectancy in Canada is 75.6 years for males and 81.7 for females (which rank in the world's longest).

*****

I have traveled to major cities in Canada from Vancouver to Nova Scotia. On visits I have gone to Uncle Tom's Cabin in Chatham at Dresden, Ontario. We visited Raleigh Township Centennial Museum, one of the few remaining Black Canadian settlements still in existence from pre-Civil War days. This museum is located in north Buxton. The North American Black Historical Museum and Cultural Centre, located in Amherstburg, contains many fascinating artifacts related to slavery as well as pioneer implements built by former slaves in Canada.

Toronto's Caribana Festival was quite an experience. It is a festival of Caribbean culture and tradition held each summer. It has been billed as North America's largest festival. If you like Mardi Gras, you will probably love the Caribana Festival. The CN Tower in downtown Toronto, Ontario, is Canada's most recognizable icon.

I was told Canadians believe in equality and diversity and respect for all individuals in society, and all women, men, children and seniors are equally respected.

MEXICO

Nickname: South of Freedom

Capital: Mexico City

Total area in sq. miles: 761,604

Most populous cities: Mexico City, Iztapalapa (The Federal District), Ecatepec (Mexico), Guadalajara (Jalisco), Ciudad Juarez (Chihuahua)

Attractions: Plaza de la Constitucion, Mexico City, Parque Alameda Central Square of the Three Cultures, Paseo de la Reform (Mexico City), Chapultepec Park (Mexico City), National Museum

345

of Anthropology (Mexico City), Museum of Natural History, the Mayan ruins at Chichen Itza, Cancun

Mexico, the United Mexican States, is a federal republic situated in North America. It is bounded on the north by the United States; on the east by the U.S., the Gulf of Mexico, and the Caribbean Sea; on the south by Belize and Guatemala; and on the west by the Pacific Ocean. Mexican federal jurisdiction extends, in addition to Mexico proper, over a number of offshore islands. The land area of the country is 761,604 sq. miles.

Most of Mexico is an immense, elevated plateau, flanked by mountain ranges that fall sharply off narrow coastal plains in the west and east. The prominent topographical feature of the country is the central plateau, a continuation of the plains of the southwestern U.S. Comprising more than half of the total area of Mexico, the plateau slopes downward from the west to the east and from the north to the south, where the elevation varies from 6,000 to

8,000 feet above sea level and where the elevation varies from about 3,500 to 4,000 feet.

Mexico has few rivers and most are not navigable. The longest river is the Rio Grande (called the Rio Bravo del Norte in Mexico), which extends along the Mexican-U.S. border. Most of Mexico lacks adequate rainfall. Rain averages less than 25 inches annually in some areas.

The mineral resources of Mexico are extremely rich and varied. Almost every known mineral can be found, including coal, iron, ore, phosphates, uranium, silver, gold, copper, lead, and zinc. Proven petroleum and natural gas reserves are enormous with some of the world's largest deposits located offshore in the Bay of Campeche. Forest and woodlands, which cover about 23% of the land, contain such valuable woods as mahogany, ebony, walnut, and rosewood. About 13% of the land is suitable for agriculture, but less than 10% receives enough rainfall for raising crops without irrigation.

The Mexican population is composed of three main groups: the people of Spanish descent, the Indians, the people of mixed Spanish and Indian ancestry, or mestizos. Of these groups, the mestizos are by far the largest, constituting about 60% of the population. The Indians total about 30%. The society is semi-industrialized.

Mexico consists of 32 administrative divisions - 31 states and the Distrito Federal (federal district), which is the seat of the federal administration.

Mexico Facts

- The official name of Mexico is the United Mexican States.
- The main language of Mexico is Spanish.
- Mexico has 68 official languages.
- Mexico is the 14th largest country by land.
- Mexico is the home of over 30 UNESCO World Heritage Sites.
- The largest source of immigration to the United States is from Mexico.

- The most popular sport in Mexico is futbol (soccer).

- It is widely believed Mexico introduced chocolate, corn, and chilies to the world.

- The first printing press in North America was used in Mexico City in 1539.

- The border between Mexico and the United States is the second largest border in the world (only the U.S.-Canadian border is longer).

- Mexico is second only to Brazil in the number of Catholic citizens.

- Mexican children do not receive presents on Christmas Day. They receive gifts on January 6, the day on which Mexicans celebrate the arrival of the Three Wise Men.

- Mexico City has the highest elevation and is the oldest city in North America. It is also one of the largest cities in the world (8.851 million people is the 2010 est.). Only ten countries have a larger population.

- Mexico is located in the "Ring of Fire" (violent earthquake and volcano zones).
- Mexico is the largest producer of silver.
- The red poinsettia originated in Mexico and is named after Joel Roberts Poinsett, the first United States Ambassador to Mexico.
- In Mexico, artists can pay their taxes with artwork.
- The world's largest pyramid is not in Egypt. The Mayan Pyramids are the largest.
- San Francisco was part of Mexico until the Mexican-American War in 1848.
- Mexico City boasts the largest taxi fleet in the world with 100,000 taxis running every day.

*****

I have visited the border towns of Juarez and Tijuana. You may want to consider visiting the pyramid at Chichen Itza in Mayan City. The ruins were evidence of an ancient city that once centered the Mayan Empire in Central America. Chichen Itza is on the World Heritage and is listed as one of the new Seven Wonders of the World by a 2007 online list of voters from around the world. Day tours leave from Cancun or Cozumel for the ruins. To date, Chichen Itza is the only site on the 2007 online list of the Seven Wonders of the World I have not visited.

CENTRAL AMERICA

Most populous cities: Guatemala City, Guatemala, Tegucigalpa, Honduras, Managua, Nicaragua

Attractions: Great Blue Hole (off Belize coast); Cocos Island (Costa Rico); Lake Atitlan (Mayan); Panama Canal; Belize Barrier Reef; Leon, Nicaragua; Copan (Mayan); Granada, Nicaragua; Panama City, Panama; Antigua, Guatemala, Ambergis Caye (Belize)

Central America is an isthmus or land bridge that unites two continents of North and South America. It consists of seven countries: Belize,

Guatemala, Honduras, El Salvador, Nicaragua, Costa Rico, and Panama. Except for Belize, all of these countries were first settled by the Spanish in the early 1500s and remained part of the Spanish colonial empire until they revolted for independence in 1821.

Geographically, the countries have a great abundance of volcanoes. This has had an important influence on the cuisine because the volcanoes have fertilized the soil with mineral nutrients that have made this one of the richest areas of biodiversity in the world. Due to this rich soil, the region has become a center of coffee production.

The population of Central America consists of four groups: mestizos, a mixture of Spanish and native peoples are the largest group; small pockets of indigenous populations; Africans; and people of unmixed European descent sometimes referred to as Creoles. Throughout much of the region, African populations are concentrated along the Atlantic coastline, while mestizos populate the Pacific side. The central area of the isthmus is home to a lush rainforest sparsely populated by small groups of indigenous tribes.

The African population descends mainly from runaway slaves who escaped from Jamaica and neighboring Caribbean islands. They have preserved a dialect of English infused with African vocabulary. This group has made Central America more diverse in language as well as in cookery, since its cooks have blended together African and indigenous food preferences. Rice is a key element in every Central American meal and is one of the important culinary contributions from Spanish cookery.

Central America Facts

- Spanish is the official language for every country with the exception of Belize, which uses English.

- You can take a central road through all of Central America with the Pan American Highway (about 30,000 miles in length).
- Located in the Ring of Fire, Central America has over 70 volcanoes.
- The Panama Canal, in Panama, is a man-made short-cut for ships sailing between the Atlantic and Pacific Oceans.
- Honduras, Panama and Costa Rico are often called "banana republics" because of the importance of bananas to their economies.
- Rice and beans go with every meal and can be every meal, including breakfast and snacking.
- The rules of the road are there are no rules.

*****

When I went to Costa Rico and Panama, we landed in San Jose and traveled to Tortuguero, where we stayed at a lodge that did not have telephone, air conditioning or television. The experience was commensurate to when I was growing up in the panhandle of Florida. My first experience riding a horse was in Costa Rico. Panama City was a real surprise. It is a modern city with a skyline that reminds one of midtown Manhattan.

In 1914, the Panama Canal joined the Atlantic and Pacific Oceans, changing international travel forever. We observed the canal use a system of locks to lift a ship 85 feet above sea level. On average, it takes 8 to 10 hours for a ship to pass through the canal. Since my visit, the canal has been expanded with a new lane of traffic due to the construction of a set of locks, increasing the waterway's capacity.

CARIBBEAN

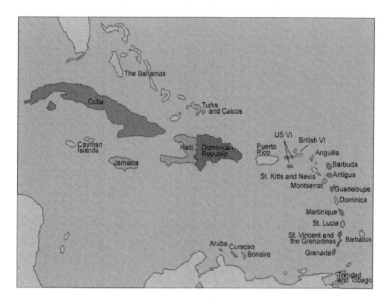

Largest countries: Cuba, Dominican Republic, Haiti, Jamaica, Trinidad and Tobago

Largest cities: Santo Domingo, Dominican Republic; Havana, Cuba; Port-au-Prince, Haiti; Kingston, Jamaica; and Santiago, Cuba

Attractions: Dunn's River Falls in Jamaica; Scenic areas in Old San Juan; Stingray City, Cayman Islands; Harrison's Caves, Barbados; Diamond Mineral Falls and Mineral Baths, St. Lucia; El

357

Yunque Rain Forest, Puerto Rico; Drive-in Volcano, La Soufriere, St. Lucia; the beaches

The Caribbean is a region that consists of the Caribbean Sea, its islands (some surrounded by the Caribbean Sea and some bordering both the Caribbean Sea and the North Atlantic Ocean), and the surrounding coasts. The region is southeast of the Gulf of Mexico and the North American mainland, east of Central America, and north of South America.

Situated largely on the Caribbean Plate, the region comprises more than 7,000 islands, islets, reefs, and caves. These islands generally form island arcs that delineate the eastern and northern edges of the Caribbean Sea. The Caribbean islands, consisting of the Greater Antilles on the north and the Lesser Antilles on the south and east (including the Leeward Antilles), are part of the somewhat larger West Indies grouping, which also includes the Lucayan Archipelago (including the Bahamas and

Turks and Caicos) north of the greater Antilles and Caribbean Sea. In a wider sense, the mainland countries of Belize, Guyana, and Suriname may be included.

The region takes its name from that of the *Caribs*, an ethnic group present in the Lesser Antilles and parts of adjacent South America at the time of the Spanish Conquest. The word "Caribbean" has multiple uses. Its principal ones are geographical and political. The Caribbean can also be expanded to include territories with strong cultural and historical connections to slavery, European colonization, and the plantation system.

Definitions of the term Greater Antilles and Lesser Antilles often vary. The Virgin Islands, as a part of the Puerto Rican Bank, are sometimes included with the Greater Antilles. The term Lesser Antilles is often used to define an island arc that includes Grenada, but excludes Trinidad and Tobago and the Leeward Antilles.

Languages spoken are Spanish, English, French, Dutch, Haitian, French Creole, English Creole, among others. There are 13 sovereign states and 17 independent territories.

The majority of the Caribbean has populations of mostly Africans in the French, Anglophone Caribbean, and Dutch Caribbean. The Spanish-speaking Caribbean has primarily mixed race, African, or European majorities. Puerto Rico has a European majority with a mixture of European-African (mulatto) and a large West African minority. One third of Cuba is of African descent, but there is a sizable mulatto (mixed African-European) population, and a European majority. The Dominican Republic has the largest mixed-race population, who descended primarily from Europeans, West Africans, and Amerindians. Larger islands, such as Jamaica, have a very large African majority in addition to significant mixed race, Chinese, Europeans, Indian, Lebanese, Latin

American, and Syrian populations. This is a result of years of importation of slaves, indentured laborers, and migration. Cuba is the largest Caribbean island, and Hispaniola is the second largest.

Island Groups

Greater Antilles

- Cuba
- Hispaniola
- Haiti
- Dominican Republic
- Jamaica
- Cayman Islands (United Kingdom)
- Puerto Rico (U.S. Commonwealth)

Lesser Antilles

- Leeward Islands
- U.S. Virgin Islands (United States)
- Saint Croix
- Saint Thomas
- Saint John

- Water Island

British Virgin Islands (United Kingdom)

- Tortola

- Virgin Gorda

- Anegada

- Jost Van Dyke

- Anguilla (United Kingdom)

- Antigua and Barbuda

- Barbuda

- Redonda

- Saint Martin (France)

- Saint Maarten (Kingdom of the Netherlands)

Saba (BES islands, Netherlands)

- Sint Eustatius (BES islands, Netherlands)

- Saint Barthelemy (French Antilles, France)

Saint Kitts and Nevis

- Saint Kitts

- Nevis

- Montserrat (United Kingdom)

Guadeloupe (French Antilles, France) including:

- Les Saintes

- Marie-Galante

- La Desirade

- Windward Islands

- Dominica

- Martinique (French Antilles, France)

- Saint Lucia

- Saint Vincent

- The Grenadines

Grenada

- Grenada

- Carriacou and Petite Martinique

- Barbados

Trinidad and Tobago

- Tobago

- Trinidad

Leeward Antilles

- Aruba (Kingdom of the Netherlands)

- Curacao (Kingdom of the Netherlands)

- Bonaire (BES islands, Netherlands)

Caribbean Facts

- There are more churches per square mile in Jamaica (1,600 in total) than in any other country in the world. According to the Guinness Book of Records, Jamaica has more churches per square mile.

- The Dominican Republic is the most visited Caribbean country, followed by Puerto Rico and Cuba.

- There are more than 21 million people that travel to the Caribbean every year. If the Caribbean were a single country, it would be the third most visited in all of the Americas, behind the United States and Mexico, and the 14th most worldwide.

- Jamaica is the largest English speaking island in the Caribbean.

- A large number of volcanoes exist in the world, but the only drive-through volcano is in the Caribbean. It is located in St. Lucia.

- More ships cruise the Caribbean islands than any other region in the world.

- Antigua has 365 beaches, one for each day of the year.

- Grenada, known as the Spice Island, has more spices per square mile than any other place in the world.

*****

I have been to several islands in the Caribbean, the first was to Nassau. I also went to the Caribbean on business when I was assigned to represent Eastern Airlines as a recruiter. One of my favorite Caribbean islands is Trinidad and Tobago. When I visited, I felt I had found my place in the sun.

June 2016, I traveled with members of Temple Zion Baptist Church, Columbia, SC, to Puerto Plata, Dominican Republic, on a short-term mission trip. The Dominican Republic is located on the island of Hispaniola. The western part of the island is occupied by Haiti, making it only one of two islands separated by two countries. Dominican Republic is the second largest nation in the Caribbean.

When I decided to go on the trip, I was not sure what to expect or how I could contribute to the mission. I have visited villages in less developed countries in Africa and knew that part of the mission would not be a culture shock, but beyond that I did not know what to expect.

Going on the mission trip allowed me to hear, touch, and see firsthand how others live. I was no longer away from the distant issues but rather "in" them. Of the different outreach experiences, one that will always standout is the visit to distribute food and other items to people living in the poorest villages near the city dump. The dump doubles as a source of food and shelter for the poorest Dominicans and Haitians, to bring them hope and a real meal. When you have choices, you have hope. Those we served during our ministry did not appear to have choices or hope.

The trip made me more aware of the global body of Christ and the needs in less developed areas. Other possible benefits of a mission trip are you will expand your limited perspective; you will become more grateful for what you have, no matter how little, and you will discover your spiritual family.

I have traveled extensively and decided I wanted to have a different experience from regular travel. The Dominican Republic mission trip will always be one of my most memorable travel experiences.

The Continents

A continent is defined as a large unbroken land mass completely surrounded by water, although in some cases continents are (or were in part) connected by land bridges. The seven continents are North America, South America, Europe, Asia, Africa, Australia, and Antarctica. In parts of the world, students learn that there are just five continents: Eurasia, Australia, Africa, Antarctica, and the Americas.

To some geographers, however, "continent" is not just a physical term; it also carries cultural connections. For example, Europe and Asia are physically part of the same landmass, but the two areas are culturally diverse. (cultural groups in Asia have more in common with one another than those in Europe.)

So, how many countries are there in the world? As of mid-2014, there were 196 nations in the world. There are 193 members of the United Nations. There are independent countries, such as Vatican City and Kosovo that are not members of the United Nations. Flags of the countries that are members of the United Nations fly outside of the U.N. Headquarters in New York City.

There are more than 15 million people who do not live on a continent. Almost all of these people live in the island countries of Oceania, a world region but not a continent.

AFRICA

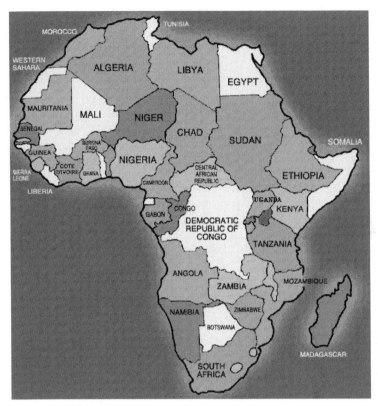

Nickname: The Dark Continent

This is the continent of wonder and the place of the evolution of human history. Africa is a continent with a diverse culture, uncountable languages, and immense natural resources. Africa is the world's second largest continent covering 20% of the earth's land and 6% of the earth's surface. It is bordered by the Atlantic Ocean to the east, the Indian Ocean to the west, and the Mediterranean Sea to the north. The Red Sea and the Suez Canal lie to the northeast and separate Africa and Asia.

The longest river in the world, The Nile, measuring 11,677,239 square miles, flows north, ending in a delta that empties into the Mediterranean Sea. The world's largest desert, The Sahara, measuring 3,500,000 miles, almost as large as the United States, covers much of North Africa. The Atlas Mountain range lies in the north-west of Africa, and the highest mountain Kilimanjaro at 19,341 feet is in Tanzania.

The countries with the largest populations are Nigeria, Egypt, Ethiopia, Democratic Republic of the Congo, and South Africa. Botswana and South Africa are the most economically developed regions while Nigeria is Africa's largest oil-producing region.

There are 53 countries in Africa: Algeria, Angola, Benin, Botswana, Burkina Faso, Burundi, Cameroon, Cape Verde, Central African Republic, Chad, Comoros, Congo (DRC), Cote d'Ivoire, Djibouti, Egypt, Equatorial Guinea, Eritrea, Gabon, Gambia, Ghana, Guinea, Guinea-Bissau, Kenya, Lesotho, Liberia, Libya, Madagascar, Malawi, Mali, Mauritania, Mauritius, Morocco, Mozambique, Namibia, Niger, Nigeria, Rwanda, Sao Tome & Principe, Senegal, Seychelles, Sierra Leone, Somalia, South Africa, Sudan, South Sudan, Swaziland, Tanzania, Togo, Tunisia, Uganda, Western Sahara, Zambia, and Zimbabwe.

Interesting Facts about Africa

- The African continent has the second largest population in the world, at about one billion.

- Well over 1,000 languages are spoken by the people of Africa. Some estimates put this number closer to two thousand.

- The oldest human remains ever discovered were found in Ethiopia. They are nearly 200,000 years old.
- Victoria Falls is the largest waterfall in Africa; it is 355 feet high and one mile wide.
- Africa is the hottest continent on earth.
- Africa is the world's second driest continent after Australia.
- Sudan is Africa's largest country (968,000 sq. miles).
- Cairo is the continent's largest city.
- The world's largest land animal is the African elephant.
- The world's tallest animal, the giraffe, lives in Africa.
- The fastest land animal in the world, the cheetah, lives in Africa.

*****

I have been to Africa five times and visited ten countries. Looking from my hotel window and seeing the Pyramids in the distance and riding a camel were thrilling experiences. We had an excellent guide from the University of Cairo who gave us the history of civilization, guided us through tombs and temples, explained the meaning of some of the hieroglyphics, and gave us more information than we could ever absorb.

Alexandria is the second largest city in Egypt extending 20 miles along the Mediterranean Sea in northern Egypt. It was founded by Alexander the Great in 331 BCE (Before the Common Era) and known as "The Pearl of the Mediterranean." It has a great lighthouse that is considered one of the Seven Wonders of the ancient world. The city grew to become the largest in the known world at the time, attracting scholars, scientists, philosophers, mathematicians, artists, and historians. The shoreline of the Mediterranean is beautiful.

We saw the Desmond Tutu House located in Soweto, an urban area of the city of Johannesburg, and the street was also the location of Nelson Mandela's previous house. The visit to Robben Island, where Nelson Mandela was imprisoned for 18 years, definitely gave us hope that we can overcome anything. My trips to Egypt and South Africa were two of my most wonderful world travel experiences.

My first safari was in Zimbabwe. Zimbabwe's main attraction is Victoria Falls. The Falls is a waterfall in southern Africa on the Zambezi River at the border of Zambia. It is classified as the largest waterfall in the world. It is twice the height of North America's Niagara Falls.

W.E.B. Du Bois is buried at the Du Bois Memorial Centre in Accra, Ghana. He was a journalist, educator, civil rights activist, and co-founder of the NAACP. He died in Accra in 1963.

Let me share that we had the ultimate cruise experience on the Nile River for three days. No other passengers were on board the ship. The cruise staff served us in a manner we were not accustomed to, but we loved it! We called ourselves the "Lucky 13." They were Boston Brice, Jr., Mary Frances Brown, Deirdre Davis, Mary Hardy, Dr. Milton Kimpson, Norma F. Myers, Beverly H. Pittman, Julia M. Martin, Holly Scott, Harriet Smedley, Amos Terry, Jr., and Helen Terry. Today we would probably call ourselves the "The Blessed 13." The experience, we felt, was equivalent to a lifestyle of the rich and famous.

ANTARCTICA

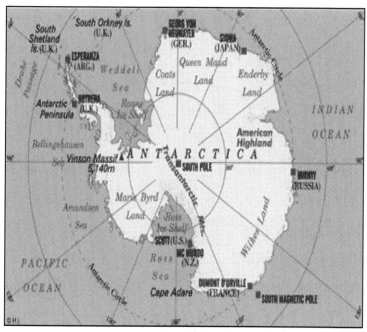

Nickname: The White Continent

Attractions: Antarctica Convergence, Antarctica Peninsula, Drake Passage, Whale-watching in the Lemaire Channel, A visit to Port Lockroy, Antactica, Antarctica Ocean, Observation Hill, Blue Ice

The continent named Antarctica is also known as the South Pole. Geographically, the southernmost part of the planet is located within its borders. In many ways Antarctica is the most unique of the seven continents geographically, with special features not shared by the others.

Antarctica is unique in that it has no permanent borders or constant size. Although it is the fifth largest continent overall, its exact size in square miles varies according to the season. The change can be quite dramatic. In the summer, the continent is roughly half the size of the United States. However, in winter when the area expands due to snow and ice, the continent can more than double in size.

One thing Antarctica has an abundance of is snow and ice; ninety-eight percent of the continent is covered in ice, and about 70% of the world's total supply of fresh water is frozen in Antarctica. No other continent is colder, drier, or windier than Antarctica, which goes a long way toward explaining another unique feature, its low population.

Antarctica has no permanent residents. Since no one lives there full time, there are no countries in Antarctica and no governments. That also means there is no form of Antarctica money in either dollars or coins. Yet, some people live and work in Antarctica on a part-time basis. These are mostly summer visitors who tend to be almost exclusively scientists conducting various forms of research. There are over 60 scientific research stations operating in Antarctica, and the total combined population of the staff of these facilities can sometimes be as high as four or five thousand. A special treaty allows anyone to use Antarctica for peaceful purposes. The most common kind of research done by visitors to Antarctica involves weather.

The highest temperature ever recorded in Antarctica is a mere 7 degrees Fahrenheit, but the coldest ever recorded is an incredible -128 degrees Fahrenheit. While Antarctica has no permanent human residents, it is home to a surprising variety of wild animals. Penguins and other birds such as the albatross can be found in Antarctica, as well as six types of seals and nine varieties of whales.

If it were not cold and covered in ice, Antarctica would be a desert much like the Sahara Desert in northern Africa because it has little yearly precipitation. Make no mistake about it, Antarctica is technically the largest desert in the world. With its extreme cold, it is unlikely that Antarctica will ever be densely populated or of much interest to humans except for scientific study.

Interesting Facts about Antarctica
- It is the only place on earth where the emperor penguins, the tallest and heaviest of all the penguins, can be found.
- It is the best place on earth to find meteorite.
- There is no time zone in Antarctica.
- Deep Lake in Antarctica is so salty it cannot freeze.

- Antarctica is the only continent without reptiles.

- Some parts of Antarctica have had no rain or snow for the last 2 million years.

- There is a waterfall in Antarctica that runs red as blood.

- There are no polar bears in Antarctica, only in the Arctic.

- Antarctica has only one ATM.

- Antarctica was once as warm as modern-day California.

*****

Four of my fellow travelers went to Antarctica in January 2015: Ervena Faulkner, Rebecca Eleazer, Ivorie Lowe, and Margie Mitchell. I decided not to go because of the weather forecast - minus 18 degrees Fahrenheit, while the average low temperature in January is similar, at about minus 21 degrees Fahrenheit.

ASIA

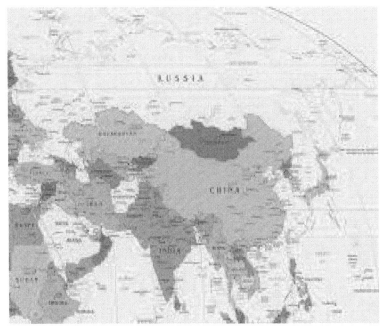

Largest countries in Asia by area: China, India, Kazakhstan

Attractions: Chiang, in Thailand; Penang, Malaysia, Singapore (shopping district); Siem Reap, in Cambodia; Forbidden City, in Beijing, China; Tokyo, Japan; Taj Mahal, Agra, in India; Victoria Peak, in Hong Kong; World Heritage Sites, in Japan; Great Wall of China (3,948 miles), Bandaling; Mount Everest, in Nepal; Mt. Fuji, in Japan; Tokyo

Tower; Tiananmen Square, in Beijing, China; Yangtze River; Terracotta Warrior Army, in Xi'an (pronounced SHE-on); Petra, Jordan; Bangkok, in Thailand; Tokyo Disney

Of all of the continents, the continent of Asia is the largest with respect to both area and population, while Australia is the smallest in both regards. The total area of the continent is 17,139,445 square miles - covering approximately 30% of the earth's land and 8.66% of the earth's surface. It is bordered by Ural Mountains to the east, the Arctic Ocean to the north, the Pacific Ocean to the west and the Indian Ocean to the south.

A large part of Russia is included in Asia, but it is also situated in Europe. For this reason it is not included in the Asian continent; otherwise, it would be the largest country in Asia. Indonesia is the largest Muslim country in the world. Singapore is one of the most developed countries in Asia and the third major tourist spot in Asia. It is also regarded as one of the cleanest and safest countries of its size.

The countries with the largest populations in Asia are China, India, Indonesia, Bangladesh, and Japan. There are 53 countries in Asia including Russia and Turkey, which lie in Europe, Asia, and Taiwan. It is technically a part of China and officially recognized as a country by the United Nations. Six hundred languages are spoken in Indonesia, eight hundred in India, more than a hundred in the Philippines, and many languages and dialects in various Chinese provinces.

The countries in Asia are Afghanistan, Armenia, Azerbaijan, Bahrain, Bangladesh, Bhutan, Brunei, Cambodia, China, Georgia, Hong Kong, India, Indonesia, Iran, Iraq, Israel, Japan, Jordan, Kazakhstan, North Korea, South Korea, Kuwait, Kyrgyzstan, Laos, Lebanon, Macau, Maldives, Malaysia, Mongolia, Myanmar, Nepal, Oman, Pakistan, Palestine, Philippines, Qatar, Russia, Saudi

Arabia, Singapore, Sri Lanka, Syria, Taiwan, Tajikistan, Timor-Leste, Turkey, Turkmenistan, United Arab Emirates, Uzbekistan, Vietnam, and Yemen.

Interesting Facts about Asia

- China and India are a third of the world's population. A total of 2.5 billion people inhabit the two countries.
- It is illegal to be fat in Japan: Japan dictates a male over 40 cannot have a waistline larger than 33.5 and a woman 35.4 inches.
- China has only one time zone; it has had only one since 1949.
- Chinese children are named after events.
- Chinese usually marry in red because white is a symbol for death.
- Paper was invented in China.
- Praising children in Jordan is taboo.
- Many shops in South Korea do not close till well after midnight.

- Nine out of ten of the world's tallest buildings are in Asia.
- Japan has the second oldest population in the world. Only Monaco has an older population.
- The longest river in Asia and the third longest in the world is the Yangtze, (3,876 miles), which flows through China.
- The largest desert in Asia is the Gobi Desert, measuring 500,000 square miles.
- The highest point in the world is Mt. Everest (29,035 feet), situated in the Tibetan region of the Himalayas.

*****

I went to the Holy Land twice. We went to Manger Square, visited the Church of the Nativity, and sailed on the "Jesus Boat" on the Sea of Galilee. We traveled to many other sites we read about in the Bible, including Armageddon, Bethlehem, Canaan, Calvary, Capernaum, Gethsemane, Golgotha,

Jericho, Jerusalem, Mt. Tabor, and Nazareth. Good things do come out of Nazareth.

Israel's Dead Sea is the lowest and saltiest spot on earth. It is bordered by Jordan to the east, and Israel and the West Bank to the west. In the Bible, it is a refuge for King David. It was one of the world's first health resorts (for Herod the Great). All in the group walked and played in the water for medicinal purposes.

The Jordan River is the only major water source flowing into the Dead Sea. The Jordan River is a river in Southeast Asia that runs along the border between Israel, the West Bank, and Jordan. Jesus was baptized by John in the Jordan River. The Jordan River is chilly and cold, but some in the group were baptized. I was in the group that waded in the water.

Beijing (formerly called Peking) is the capital of the People's Republic of China, and it is one of the most populous cities in the world. We were there before they hosted the 2008 Summer Olympics. At the city center is the Palace that was built for the Heavenly Emperor. It is also called the Forbidden City because permission was needed from the emperor to enter. Now known as the Palace Museum, it is north of Tiananmen Square. Thousands of people come to the Square every day.

Shanghai is the country's most populous city and is the most populous city in the world. Air pollution is a serious health problem in Shanghai. The pollution was so intense I had to cover my nose. Hong Kong is a Special Administrative Region of the People's Republic of China. It has the most skyscrapers in the world.

It was a very hot summer day, but I walked up many of the steps of the Great Wall of China. The Wall was built during the Ming Dynasty (1368-1644) to repeal foreign influences and exert control over its citizens. It is one of the world's most famous landmarks.

After traveling to India, I said I should never complain again about what I do not have. We saw what appeared to be millions of people who live in conditions you can never imagine. India is second to China in having the most people in the world.

The Taj Mahal, originally built by Emperor Shah Jahan to house the tomb of his wife, opened in 1648 in Agra and remains one of the world's most celebrated structures. It is a stunning structure and was designated a UNESCO World Heritage Site in 1983. Some say it is the most beautiful building in the world. It is definitely the most magnificent building I have ever seen.

We visited the Raj Ghat Memorial of Mahatma Gandhi ("Great Soul") in New Delhi. Gandhi was leader of India's independence movement and was the architect of a form of non-violent civil disobedience. Gandhi's actions inspired Dr. Martin Luther King, Jr., and Nelson Mandela.

We had a mountain-top experience when we flew near Mount Everest, the tallest mountain on earth (29,035 ft.), on August 6, 2013. It is five and one-half miles above sea level, which is equivalent to the size of almost 20 Empire State Buildings. Approximately 4,000 people have attempted to climb Mount Everest since Sir Edmund Hillary and Sherpa Tenzing Norgay in 1953. Only 660 or more have been successful. Over 280 people have died trying to climb Mt. Everest. It is a part of the Himalaya Mountain range that straddles the borders of Nepal and Tibet.

For those who like tall mountains, as I do, the six other summits, from highest to lowest, are as follows:

1. South America: Aconcagua 22,829 ft.
2. North America: Denali 20,320 ft.

3. Africa: Kilimanjaro 19,340 ft.

4. Europe: Mt. Elbrus 18,510 ft.

5. Antarctica: Mt. Vinson 16,067 ft.

6. Australia: Mt. Kosciuszko 7,310

AUSTRALIA

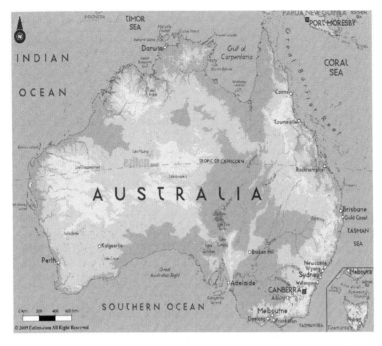

Nickname: Aussie, The Land Down Under

Capital: Canberra

Attractions: Sydney Opera House, Harbour Highlights cruises, Jenolan Caves, the Marine Aquarium at Darling Harbor, Perth, Tasmania, Fraser Island, Kakadu National Park (World Heritage Site), Uluru (largest monolith rock in the world), Kangaroo Island, Jamison Valley, Great Barrier Reef, Sydney Harbor Bridge, Blue

Mountains National Park (World Heritage Site), Melbourne, Bondi Beach, Daintree National Park (World Heritage Site), Broome, and the Kimberley region

Australia is the world's smallest continent, only 2,967,909 square miles, but it is a highly diverse continent. While Australia may be small compared to other continents, it is the sixth largest country in the world in land mass. Australia, also called Australasia/Oceania, covers approximately 5.3% of the earth's land and 1.5% of the earth's surface. Australia is the only country that is a continent. It is called "down under" because it is on the other side of the world in the Southern Hemisphere.

The country is situated partly in the Pacific Ocean, bordered by the Indian Ocean to the west and the Southern ocean to the south. Australia is the flattest continent with much of Australia being desert. Australia/Oceania is the least populated continent after Antarctica. It contains around 0.5%

of the world's population with a growth rate of approximately 1.35 percent per year.

The countries with the largest populations are Australia, Papua New Guinea, New Zealand, and Fiji. The most populated city in Australia is Sydney, followed closely by Melbourne. The 28 countries and island groups in Australia/Oceania are Australia, Christmas Island, Comoros Islands, Cook Islands, Fiji, Guam, Kiribati, Marshall Islands, Federated States of Micronesia, Nauru, New Caledonia, New Zealand, Nauru, Norfolk Islands, Northern Mariana Islands, Palau, Papua New Guinea, Pitcairn Islands, French Polynesia, America Samoa, Solomon Islands, Tokelau, Tonga, Tuvalu, Vanuatu, and Wallis and Futuna.

Interesting Facts about Australia

- There are more sheep living in Australia than people.

- Australia is one of the wealthiest and safest nations in the world.
- Australia was the second country in the world to give women the right to vote in 1902 (New Zealand was the first).
- Canberra was selected the capital because residents in Sydney and Melbourne could not stop arguing about which city should be the capital of Australia.
- Australia is the biggest island in the world.
- In Australia, there are more kangaroos than people.
- In Victoria, Australia, only a licensed electrician is allowed to change a light bulb.
- Australia has over 10,000 beaches. You could visit a new beach every day for over 27 years.

*****

A trip to Australia was not on my bucket list, but it was on the list of the twenty-four people who traveled with me, so I went. While there were several, one of the major highlights for me was the tour and performance at the iconic Sydney Opera House. In case you decide to go and depending on where you reside, the distance from Dallas/Fort Worth to Sydney is 8,108 miles and seventeen hours five minutes flying time. Emirates' new flight from Dubai to Auckland - which lasts seventeen hours and fifteen minutes - officially became the world's longest nonstop scheduled commercial route.

When we left Australia, we went to the beautiful island of Fiji in the South Pacific. Fiji was another one of my favorite places in the sun. It became independent in 1970, after nearly a century as a British colony. Fiji Island comprises 332 in the South Pacific and has a population of 903,207 (2013 est.).

EUROPE

Attractions: The Eiffel Tower, in Paris; Acropolis, in Athens, Greece; The Colosseum, in Rome; Edinburgh Castle, in Scotland; Sagrada Familia, in Barcelona, Spain; Buckingham Palace, in United Kingdom; Lourve, in Paris; Notre Dame de Paris, in Paris; Vatican City, in Rome; Stonehenge, in

Wiltshire, England; Ann Frank House, in Amsterdam

Europe is the second smallest continent, covering approximately 6.7% of the earth's land and 25% of the earth's surface. It is bordered by the Atlantic to the west, the Arctic Ocean to the north, the Mediterranean Sea to the south, and ending in the Ural Mountains in Russia. The longest river in Europe is the Volga, measuring approximately 2,300 miles. Europe is the third most populated continent with about 11% of the world's population. The countries with the highest population are Russia, Germany, United Kingdom, France, and Italy. Russia is the largest country in Europe, and Vatican City with a population as low as 800 people is the smallest.

There are 47 countries in Europe, including Russia and Turkey which lie in both Europe and Asia. The countries are Albania, Andorra, Austria, Belarus, Belgium, Bosnia and Herzegovina,

Bulgaria, Croatia, Cyprus, Czech Republic, Denmark, Estonia, Finland, France, Germany, Greece, Hungary, Iceland, Ireland, Italy, Latvia, Liechtenstein, Lithuania, Luxembourg, Macedonia, Malta, Moldova, Monaco, Montenegro, Netherlands, Norway, Poland, Portugal, Romania, Russia, San Marino, Serbia, Slovakia, Spain, Sweden, Switzerland, Turkey, Ukraine, United Kingdom, and Vatican City.

Interesting Facts about Europe

- London's underground escalators travel a distance that equals 2 trips around the world each week.

- The Leaning Tower of Pisa took nearly 200 years to build.

- Brussels airport sells more chocolate than anywhere else in the world.

- The original croissant was, in fact, invented in Austria.

- The Statue of Liberty was built in France.

- The Mediterranean was a desert.

*****

My first visit to Europe was in the winter to Denmark, Sweden, England, France, and Germany. Copenhagen is a city of canals, rivers and parks. One of Copenhagen's most famous attractions is Tivioli Gardens, which has an amusement park and other attractions. A lesson I learned in Sweden was from a taxi driver. I did not study the currency before arriving, and he told me in a direct way I better learn. The moral of the story is to have an elementary knowledge of the local currency before you travel to the country. While the Scandinavian countries were cold and appeared dreary, studies indicate the Danes are one of the happiest group of people on the planet. I saw the usual tourist attractions in London and visited several castles in Germany on different tours.

I have been to eighteen countries in Europe, but my favorites are The Netherlands (Amsterdam),

Italy (Rome), and The Vatican. Amsterdam is a picturesque and vibrant city. It is the largest city and capital of The Netherlands. There are over a million bikes within the city limits, yet only about 700,000 people. It appears that almost everyone rides a bicycle in Amsterdam. The question is, why so many cyclists? It may be because riding a bike is fast, cheap, healthy, and easy because there are no hills to climb. Flowers are a big business in Holland. The Dutch are leading world exporters of flowers. Amsterdam has more canals than Venice. Half of the land is below sea level.

Rome is regarded as one of the world's most beautiful and ancient cities, and it contains vast amounts of priceless works of art, palaces, museums, parks, churches, gardens, basilicas, and temples. Rome is a city of monuments - a lot of them. Nude statues are common in Roman art. The Colosseum is the most visited place in Rome. When we were there, we tried to "do as the Romans," such as toss coins in Trevi Fountain. If you go, be prepared to mingle with a beehive of people.

St. Peter's Square, located in Vatican City, can host more than 200,000 people. The dome of St. Peter's Basilica was designed by Michelangelo. His famous Sistine Ceiling depicts scenes from Genesis.

Florence is a stunning province of hills and mountains. Among its famous sons are Leonardo da Vinci, Dante, Machiavelli, and Michelangelo. The main attraction in Pisa is the 14th century Romanesque Leaning Tower. Galileo developed his laws of gravity while in Florence.

Venice, Italy, has over 150 canals, over 118 islands, and over 400 bridges. Among its top attractions is a romantic Gondola ride.

The Eiffel Tower in Paris is another one of the most recognizable structures on the planet. It was constructed in 1889 as the entrance to the World's Fair. At 1,063 feet, it is about the same height as an

81-story building. It is the tallest structure in Paris and is one of the most visited sites in the world.

The Louvre is the world's largest and most visited museum. It is a city within a city, a vast multi-leveled maze of galleries, passageways, staircases, and escalators. The IM Pei glass pyramid entrance is a wonderful piece of architecture. Let's not forget the ever so famous masterpieces: the Venus of Milo, the Winged Victory of Samothrace, the Mona Lisa of Leonard da Vinci (the painting is over 500 years old), and so many more.

Whether one of the reasons you travel to Belgium is for waffles, know there are several kinds, including the Brussel waffle and the Liege waffle, none of them called Belgian.

When you say, "It looks like Greek to me," it will ring true when you visit Greece. Greece is strategically located at the crossroads of Europe, Asia, and Africa. It has more international airports because of the number of foreign visitors. The Parthenon on top of the Acropolis is one of the most famous Greek tourist attractions, and a visit to Athens is not complete without visiting this temple. During its lifetime, the Parthenon has served as a temple, fortress, a church, a mosque, and even a powder magazine.

I took a short lap on the track of the 1896 Athens Olympic Stadium, where the first Olympic Games began 120 years ago, and cruised to the Greek islands of Aegina, Hydra, Poros.

NORTH AMERICA

Attractions: Niagara Falls, in Ontario, Canada; Washington, DC; Banff National Park, in Alberta, Canada; Walt Disney World, in FL; Grand Canyon, in AZ; Yosemite National Park, in WY; Historic Quebec City, in Canada; Golden Gate Bridge, in CA; Tenochtitlan, in Federated District in Mexico; Arlington National Cemetery, in VA: CN Tower, in

Toronto, in Canada; Old Montreal, Canada; US Capitol Building, in Washington, DC; White House, in Washington, DC; Willis (Sears) Tower, in Chicago; National Memorial, in Oklahoma City, OK; Notre-Dame-de-Quebec Basilica-Cathedral; Denali National Park, in AK; Las Vegas, NV Strip; Florida Keys; Manhattan

North America is the third largest continent of the seven continents with respect to area while being the most populous continent after Asia and Africa. It shares its border with the Atlantic Ocean to the east and Pacific Ocean to the west. Canada, USA, and Mexico are the most dominant countries in the North American continent. The Mississippi-Missouri is the longest river in North America and the fourth largest in the world. Its length is approximately 3,600 miles. Mount Denali (20,322 ft.) in Alaska is the tallest point on this continent, and Death Valley in California is the lowest point. Economically, this continent is comprised of the world's most developed nations like Canada, USA, and Mexico.

The most populous countries in North America are the United States, Mexico, Canada, Guatemala, and Cuba. Countries in North America are Antigua and Barbuda, Bahamas, Barbados, Belize, Canada, Costa Rico, Cuba, Dominica, Dominican Republic, El Salvador, Greenland, Grenada, Guatemala, Haiti, Honduras, Jamaica, Mexico, Nicaragua, Panama, Saint Kitts and Nevis, Saint Lucia, Saint Vincent and The Grenadines, Trinidad and Tobago, and the United States of America. There are 23 countries in North America and several possessions and territories.

Interesting Facts about North America

- Most North Americans speak English, Spanish, or French.
- Mexico City, Mexico, is the largest city in North America.

- North America is the only continent that has every kind of a climate.

- North America was named after the Italian explorer Amerigo Vespucci.

- Mexico is the poorest country in North America. The United States is the wealthiest.

- The first written constitution of the world is that of the United States.

- Canada has the highest number of lakes in the world.

- The busiest railway junction of the world is the Chicago Railway Junction.

- Every drop of water that falls on two-thirds of the United States from New York to Yellowstone flows from the Mississippi River.

- The world's shortest river is the Roe River (201 ft.) near Great Falls, Montana, USA.

- The coldest place in North America is Greenland; it can get to -87 degrees Fahrenheit.

- The world's busiest inland waterway is the St. Lawrence River.

- Niagara Falls in North America is one of the most popular waterfalls in the world.

- The country of Greenland is the biggest island on the planet.

*****

Intentionally left blank for you to fill in comments on North America.

SOUTH AMERICA

Attractions: Machu Picchu, in Peru; Amazonia, in Ecuador; Angel Falls, in Venezuela; The Galapagos Islands, in Ecuador; Rio de Janeiro, in Brazil; Iguazu Falls, Argentina-Brazil; Christ the Redeemer, in Rio de Janeiro, Brazil

The continent of South America is situated between the Pacific and Atlantic Oceans. A good number of people from various non-English speaking countries do not accept the idea of it being a continent in the true sense of the term. They regard North, Central, and South America as subcontinents. The great Amazon River that surrounds a vast area of Amazon forests is located in South America. Andes, the second largest mountain range in the world after the Himalayas, also run down the western edge of South America. The largest salt lake in the world is located in Bolivia. Portuguese and Spanish are the major languages of South America. A considerable gap between rich and poor is quite evident. The richest countries like Venezuela, Brazil, and Paraguay might own 60% of the total nation's wealth, while the poorest may own less than 5%.

The most populous countries in South America are Brazil, Colombia, Argentina, Peru, and

Venezuela. The continent is comprised of 12 independent countries including Argentina, Bolivia, Brazil, Chile, Colombia, Ecuador, Guyana, Paraguay, Peru, Suriname, Uruguay, Venezuela, and the overseas department of French Guiana. South America is ranked fourth in area and fifth in population.

Interesting Facts about South America

- South America has the largest rain forest in the world, the Amazon Rain Forest.
- Brazil is larger than China and slightly smaller than the USA.
- South America is connected to North America by a narrow strip of land called Isthmus of Panama.
- The Amazon River carries more water than any other river on earth; it is so large it can be seen from outer space.

In summary, the largest continents in area are Asia, Africa, North America, South America, Antarctica, Europe, and Australia.

*****

Of the four South America countries I have visited, Brazil is my favorite. The exquisite Iguazu Falls are magnificent. Today, the Iguazu Falls are owned by the two UNESCO World Heritage Sites: the Iguazu National Park in Argentina and the Iguacu National Park in Brazil.

Rio de Janeiro is famed for its glorious beaches Copacabana and Ipanema. Ipanema immortalized in the 1960 famous bossa nova hit, "The Girl from Ipanema," is Rio's most sophisticated beach. Go to Corcovado Mountains and see the statue of Christ the Redeemer, which is one of the Seven Wonders of the World.

"The best part of the journey may be the people we meet on the way." --Author Unknown

World Heritage Sites

A World Heritage Site is a place (such as a forest, mountain, lake, desert, monument, building, complex, or city) that is listed by the United Nations Educational and Cultural Organization (UNESCO) as having a special cultural or physical significance. The list is maintained by the International World Heritage Programme which is administered by the UNESCO World Heritage Committee, composed of 21 state parties which are elected by the General Assembly.

The program catalogues, names, and conserves sites of outstanding cultural or natural importance to the common heritage of humanity. As of 2015, 1007 sites are listed: 779 cultural, 197 natural, and 31 mixed properties in 161 state parties. A few of the 21 World Heritage Sites in the United States include the Everglades National Park, in Florida; Grand Canyon in Arizona; Great Smoky Mountains, in eastern Tennessee and western North Carolina; Independence Hall, in Philadelphia; Statue of Liberty, in New York; and Yellowstone National Park, in Wyoming, Montana, and Idaho (96% of Yellowstone is in Wyoming).

Some familiar World Heritage Sites are Rio de Janeiro, in Brazil; Pyramids of Giza, in Egypt; Robben Island, in South Africa; Great Wall, in China; Taj Mahal, in India; Sydney Opera House, in Australia; Venice, Italy, and Vatican City.

Oceans

The oceans cover 71 percent of the Earth's surface and contain 97 percent of the planet's water. There are five oceans: Antarctic, Arctic, Atlantic, Indian, and Pacific. All oceans are connected and who can say where one ocean stops and the next ocean starts.

The Pacific Ocean is the largest. It is the biggest ocean on earth with an area of 63.78 million square miles. It is also bigger than all of the land on the planet put together. It borders four continents: North America, South America, Australia, and Asia.

The Atlantic Ocean is the second largest. It covers 20% of the Earth's entire surface. All of the Central and South American countries on the Caribbean Sea, including Cuba, Jamaica, Panama, Colombia, Venezuela, and the United States, and many others have an Atlantic coast, as well as the South American countries of Argentina and Brazil.

The Indian Ocean is the third largest. It makes up about 20% of the Earth's water. Named after the country of India, it is bordered by Asia to the north, Antarctica to the south, Australia to the east, and Africa to the west.

The Antarctic Ocean, also known as the Southern Ocean, is an enormous body of water that surrounds the entire continent of Antarctica and reaches Australia and the southern end of South America.

The Arctic Ocean is the smallest and shallowest of the world's oceans. Covering approximately 5,427,000 square miles, the body of water is approximately the size of Russia. Due to its cold temperature, part of the ocean remains covered by ice throughout the year.

Deepest Parts of the Ocean

Location	Ocean	Depth
Mariana Trench	Pacific Ocean	35,827 feet (6.8 miles)
Puerto Rico Trench	Atlantic Ocean	30,246 feet (5.7 miles)
Java Trench	Indian Ocean	24,460 feet (4.6 miles)
Arctic Basin	Arctic Ocean	18,456 feet (3.5 miles)

Note: An airplane flying at 33,000 feet is 6.2 miles above you - so imagine the same sort of distance below and you have the Mariana Trench.

Seven Wonders of The World

Since ancient times, numerous "seven wonders" lists have been created. The contents of these lists tend to vary, and none is definitive. The seven wonders that are most widely agreed upon as being on the original list are **Seven Wonders of the Ancient World,** which was compiled by ancient Greek historians and is thus confined to the most magnificent structures known to the ancient Greek world. Of all the Ancient Wonders, the Pyramids survived.

On July 7, 2007, an organization announced a "new" set of Seven Wonders of the World based on online voting from around the globe. On this list are the following:

- Chichen Itza, Mexico - Mayan City
- Christ Redeemer, Brazil - Large Statue
- The Great Wall of China
- Machu Picchu, Peru

- Petra, Jordan - Ancient City
- The Roman Colosseum - Italy
- The Taj Mahal - India

Another list was announced in 1997 by CNN that include the following:

- Grand Canyon, Arizona
- The Great Barrier Reef - Northeast coast of Australia's state of Queensland
- The Harbor - Rio de Janeiro, Brazil
- Mt. Everest - World's highest mountain located on the border of Nepal and Tibet, China (Tibet is part of China)
- Northern Lights - Seen near Arctic Circle in Alaska, Canada and Norway
- Paricutin Volcano - State of Michoacán, Mexico
- Victoria Falls - Zambia and Zimbabwe border in Africa

In 1994, the American Society of Civil Engineers decided to put together a list of the most remarkable civil engineering feats of the 20th century. The seven selected projects are a tribute to the greatest works of the modern world. They are as follows:

- Channel Tunnel - Under the English Channel
- CN Tower - Toronto, Canada
- Empire State Building - New York City
- Golden Gate Bridge - San Francisco, CA
- Itaipu Dam - Between Brazil and Paraguay
- Panama Canal - Connects Atlantic Ocean with the Pacific Ocean
- Netherlands North Sea Protection Works - Prevents flooding during storms in Netherlands and Europe

Geographic Superlatives

Largest in Area	Smallest in Area
Russia	Vatican City
North America: Canada	North America: St. Kitts and Nevis
South America: Brazil	South America: Suriname
Europe: Russia (Ukraine is the largest.)	Europe: Vatican City (country entirely in Europe)
Asia: Russia (China is the largest.)	Asia: Maldives (entirely in Asia)
Africa: Algeria	Africa: Seychelles
Australia/Oceania: Australia	Australia/Oceania: Nauru

Largest in Population	Smallest in Population
China	Vatican City
North America United States	North America: St. Kitts and Nevis
South America: Brazil	South America: Suriname
Europe: Russia (Germany is the most)	Europe: Vatican City (populated country entirely in Europe)
Asia: China	Asia: Maldives
Africa: Nigeria	Africa: Seychelles
Australia/Oceania: Australia	Australia/Oceania: Tuvalu

Note: Six of the smallest countries are island nations.

Ten Largest Countries	Ten Smallest Countries
1. Russia	1. Maldives
2. Canada	2. Seychelles
3. United States	3. Saint Kitts and Nevis
4. China	4. Marshall Islands
5. Brazil	5. Liechtenstein
6. Australia	6. Marino
7. India	7. Tuvalu
8. Argentina	8. Nauru
9. Kazakhstan	9. Monaco
10. Algeria	10. Vatican City

Highest Point	Lowest Point
Mount Everest: (Nepal/ China)	Dead Sea (Israel/ Jordan)
North America: Mount Denali (U.S.)	North America: Death Valley (U.S.)
South America: Aconcagua (Argentina)	South America: Laguna del Carbon (Argentina)
Europe: Mount Elbrus (Russia)	Europe: Caspian Sea (Russia)
Asia: Mount Everest (Nepal/China)	Asia: Dead Sea (Israel/Jordan)
Africa: Kilimanjaro (Tanzania)	Africa: Lake Assal (Djibouti)
Australia/Oceania: Mt. Wilhelm (Papua New Guinea)	Australia/Oceania: Lake Eyre (Australia)

Longest River	Largest Lake
Antarctica: Onyx River	Antarctica: Lake Vostok
North America: Mississippi-Missouri	North America: Lake Superior (U.S./Canada)
South America: Amazon	South America: Lake Titicaca (Peru/Bolivia)
Europe: Volga	Europe: Caspian Sea (Russia/Lake Ladoga (Russia) is the largest lake entirely in Europe.
Asia: Change Jiang (Yangtze)	Asia: Caspian Sea (Azerbaijan/Iran/Turkmenistan/Kazakhstan) Lake Baikal (Russia) is the largest lake entirely in Asia.
Africa: Nile	Africa: Lake Victoria (Kenya/Tanzania/Uganda)
Australia/Oceania: Murray-Darling	Australia/Oceania: Lake Eyre (Australia)

Largest island: Greenland

Largest desert: Sahara (Africa)

Largest rain forest: Amazon (South America)

Largest swamp: Pantanal (South America)

Most populated city: Shanghai (24,150,000)

Least populated city: Vatican City (population 842 people) (Smallest city and state in world)

Wealthiest city: Tokyo, Japan

Poorest country: Kinshasa, Congo (Many residents live on less than a $1 a day.)

Most expensive city: Singapore

Least expensive city to live in: Mumbai, India

Wettest spot on earth: Mawsynram, India

Driest spot on earth: Atacama Desert (averages 467 inches of rain per year) South America (averages 4 inches of rain every 100 years.)

World's oldest city: Damascus, Syria

World' youngest country: South Sudan (Independence recognized 2011)

"Traveling is designed to inspire, enrich and educate."

--Author Unknown

Epilogue

A goal in writing this guide is to give a worldview of places you can go when you travel. When I was growing up in a rural community in the panhandle of Florida, I did not know these places and countries ever existed. My first ah-ha travel moment came after my freshman year of college when I went to New York to work for the summer in the garment district. While my exposure to places outside of my birthplace came late in life, I am glad to see so many young people who go on school field trips, college tours, and college students who intern and study abroad, etc., which is now the norm for many and not the exception. Travel is educational and broadens one's horizon and perspective.

Patricia Schultz wrote a traveler's life list of *1,000 Places to See Before You Die* - on and off the beaten path; that's a lot of places. I met a traveler in Alaska who claimed she had visited seventy-five countries, and her goal was to travel to one hundred; that's a lot of countries. John Kerry was the most traveled U.S. Secretary of State, logging in more than a million air miles. From 2009-2013 Hillary Clinton visited the most countries, 112. She traversed 956,733 miles - enough to span the globe more than 38 times. While this guide covers places in the United States and world to see, you do not have to start your travel experience by going to exotic and distant places. I maintain that you can begin adding to your travel experiences by taking a one-day, two or three-day trip to places close to where you live. You will be amazed at the interesting places close to home, and do not cost a lot to get there.

When I initially began planning trips for the Ridgewood Foundation, I planned randomly and did not have a purpose for the tours. After a while the light shined, and I had a better sense of how to plan. So, when you travel, you may want to concentrate on seeing theme parks, museums, national parks, beaches, all states in the United States, state capitals, mountain ranges, monuments, memorial statutes, presidential libraries, African American sites, iconic bridges, golf courses, sports arenas, botanical gardens, places on the superlatives list, or research places and sites listed to increase your knowledge. The list of possible areas is endless and does not end here; it only begins here.

I watch Jeopardy on television and often hear a contestant state that his/her goal is to travel to all fifty states or all the state capitals. One of the goals for my groups was to see state capitals, colleges, universities, and African-American sites. By the way, this guide will not help you become a contestant on Jeopardy, but to Jeopardy fans, there are many questions on geography contained herein that may be asked on Jeopardy.

There is one travel program on television that still fascinates me: "On the Road" with Steve Hartman. One of my all-time favorite television travel features no longer shown was "Where in the World Is Matt (Lauer)?" These programs helped me travel vicariously or inspired me to plan travel to some of the locations. The Scandinavian author and poet Hans Christian Andersen once wrote, "To move, to breathe, to fly, to float, to gain all while you give, to roam the roads of lands remote, to travel is to live."

I hope after reading this travel book, you will be inspired to travel somewhere, even if it is to an interesting place in your city or state you know about but have not visited. You will be surprised what you will learn or how you may be inspired.

"The best part of the journey may be the people we meet on the way." --Author Unknown

431

When you travel, remember the

Ten Commandments for All Travelers:

I. Thou shall not expect to find things as thou have them at home, for thou have left home to find things different.

II. Thou shall not take anything too seriously...for a carefree mind is the beginning of a good vacation.

III. Thou shall not let the other tourists get on thy nerves...for thou art paying out good money to have a good time.

IV. Remember thou passport (when traveling outside the U.S.) so that thou knowest where it is at all times, for a man without a passport is a man without a country.

V. Blessed is the man who can make change in any language...and lo he shall not be cheated.

VI. Blessed is the man who can say "thank you" in any language...and it shall be worth more to him than many tips.

432

VII. Thou shall not worry. He that worrieth has no pleasure and very few things are ever fatal.

VIII. Thou shall, when in Rome, do somewhat as the Romans do; if in difficulty, thou shall use American common sense and friendliness.

IX. Thou shall not judge the people of a country by one person with whom thou has had trouble.

X. Remember thou art a guest in every land...and he that treateth his host with respect shall be treated as an honored guest.

As long as it is physically possible, visit places you wish to visit because life ends when you stop dreaming, do not have hope, or do not have anything to look forward to. I think the following is very beautiful, and I want to share it with you.

At birth we boarded the train of life and met our parents, and we believed they would always travel on by our side. However, at some station our parents will step down from the train, leaving us on this journey alone. As time goes by, other people will board the train, and they will be significant, i.e., our siblings, friends, the love of our life, and even our children. Many will step down and leave a permanent vacuum. Others will go unnoticed, and we do not realize they vacated their seats. This train will be full of joy, sorrow, fantasy, expectations, hellos, goodbyes, and farewells. Success consists of having a good relationship with all passengers, requiring that we give the best of ourselves.

The mystery to everyone is: We do not know at which station we ourselves will step down. So, we must live in the best way, love, forgive, and offer the best of who we are. It is important to do this because when the time comes for us to step down and leave our seat empty, we should leave behind beautiful memories for those who will continue to travel on the train of life.

I wish you a joyful journey on the train of life, and the best for much success. In addition, give lots of love. When you see the beauty of America and the wonders of the world, you will see how "God shed His grace on thee." More importantly, be thankful for your journey - I am. Lastly, I thank you for being one of the passengers on my train. Happy Traveling!

About the Author

Photo by Beverly H. Pittman

Ezell Pittman, PhD

Ezell Pittman, PhD, enjoys planning domestic and international travel for groups, serving as an adjunct professor at Webster University, and assisting students who seek higher education goals. He resides in Columbia, SC. For more information, contact him via e-mail at ezpitt3@netscape.net.

Made in the USA
Columbia, SC
01 August 2017